brew
think up
craft
conceive
fabricate
create
imagine
emerge
bear
develop
concoct
plan
dream

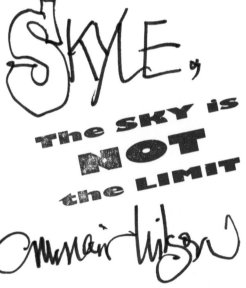

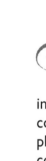

HATCH!

invent
contrive
plot
conspire
parturition
devise
birth
spitball
idealize
calve
dream
reproduce
propose
foal
discover
produce
make up
percolate
concoct

ENDORSEMENTS

{applause}

CRAIG MCNAiR WiLson is A
Triple-sTrenGTH MotivATor,
A WATerFAll of creAtivity and
HUMor, and A remArkable
iNnoVAtor. He is THe ModerN-DAy
LeonArdo DA ViAci

SARK AuTHor/Artist
Succulent WiLD WoMan
and MaNy oTHer Books
www.cAMpSARK.com

"McNair Wilson's presentation on creativity is one of the most dynamic, profound, and enjoyable I have ever heard. McNair's delivery, theatrics, staging, and all-around presentation skills are nothing short of masterful. His content is unmatched—he knows his stuff from experience. As somebody who has watched, studied, and coached speakers for years, this man is one of the very best I have ever witnessed."
Patricia Fripp, Past President, National Speakers Assoc.,
Co-author, *Speaking Secrets of the Masters*

"I am always careful not to overstate things and I am connected to a lot of creative people. No one I know is more creative than McNair Wilson. I use him a lot—whenever I can—relating to our Christian Writers Guild speaking, motivating, coaching. He has spoken many times at my national and regional conferences, and he has personally coached me. I have used him for our full staff retreat as well. I recommend him with enthusiasm and without reservation. He won't disappoint."
Jerry B. Jenkins, Author, Speaker

"McNair is a force of nature. He has a passion to help people be all they can be. Engaging and inspiring, our senior staff was talking about him for weeks. We have had him back year after year. He's a pleasure to work with."
Wendell Burton (For the Executive Staff), Lakewood Church, Houston, Texas

"Since we began to apply McNair Wilson's creative thinking techniques on a national basis, we have blown the lid off of our sales! And our customer satisfaction has never been higher. We have used him year-after-year to train and inspire our executive team and sales staff."
Marc McBride, CEO, McBride Electric National

"McNair, I watched Mr. Holland's Opus (you sent me) twice—just as good both times. I am reminded that success is not measured by the money you make or the awards you accumulate. Success is measured by the lives you touch. In that regard you, my friend, are the Donald Trump of a generation of artists and communicators."
Ken Davis, Speaker, Humorist :: Author, *Secrets of Dynamic Communications*
Founder, Dynamic Communicator's Workshops

"In all my years with National Speakers Association, I have never seen anyone receive a standing ovation as long as the one afforded McNair Wilson at our San Francisco conference. He moved and inspired an audience of more than three hundred professional speakers in a way that has not occurred before. He is a true inspiration."
Gary C. Purece, Past President,
National Speakers Assoc., N. Calif. chapter

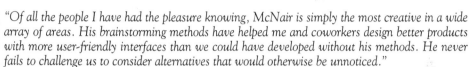

"Of all the people I have had the pleasure knowing, McNair is simply the most creative in a wide array of areas. His brainstorming methods have helped me and coworkers design better products with more user-friendly interfaces than we could have developed without his methods. He never fails to challenge us to consider alternatives that would otherwise be unnoticed."
Bill Griffis, Solutions Architect at Front Range Solutions,
IT Leadership at The Navigators

"While some of us vacation in the land of Creativity, McNair has taken up permanent residence and leads sight-seeing tours through that marvelous, wonderful, and magical place. I can think of no better guide through brainstorms and the land of unlocked creativity than McNair Wilson."
Kurt Birky, Global Brand Director, Compassion International

"McNair is an experienced teacher and performer who uses humor, creativity, and insights that are bold and just a little bit wacky. He appeals to all ages—teens, collegians, and professionals. His use of rich theatrical experiences and techniques makes him a great fit for large business gatherings. We in the Salvation Army have used him all over the country at a wide variety of conferences. Best of all, his contagious joy lets everyone know that to be a Christian is never to be bored or boring."
Maj. Carl Ruthberg, Conference Center Director, The Salvation Army - USA East

"Great speaker. Great person. Witty and wise."
Allen Klein, Author, *The Healing Power of Humor* and other books
President, The Association for Applied and Therapeutic Humor

"I have worked with McNair Wilson in some of the most demanding of creative circumstances. No one compares with McNair for the grand creative gesture or the sheer g-force of ideas that come the way of anything to which he gives his attention. He can, and will, do whatever is necessary without attitude, and yet he is capable of delegating to and engaging even the toughest of coworkers. The term "renaissance man" is employed all too often, unfortunately, because it ought to be saved for the rare man like McNair. The years of our varied collaborations and the ongoing friendship that has ensued is its own highest endorsement."
Lauralee Farrer, President, Burning Heart Productions
(Producer, *Cyrano de Begerac*, presented by Theatre Quest, Directed by McNair Wilson)

"Most of life's failures are people who did not realize how close they were to success when they gave up." Thomas Edison

HATCH!

BRAINSTORMING

SECRETS OF A THEME PARK DESIGNER

Written & Illustrated by

C. McNAIR WILSON

Former Ɗısɴ℮ɏ Imagineer

BookVillages

HATCH!

BOOK VILLAGES and the BOOK VILLAGES logo are registered trademarks of Book Villages. Absence of ® in connection with the marks of Book Villages or other parties does not indicate an absence of registration of those marks.

ISBN: 978-1-93851-201-8

Cover design by Kemper Simpich and McNair Wilson
Interior design by Niddy Griddy Design, Inc.
Author photo, back cover: MaxPaul Franklin

Illustrations by C. McNair Wilson
Additional art: Steve Björkman (165,192); Gus Dijon (196); Clark Tate (61, 62, 198); used by permission
Spot art (old advertising art by Lewis Hymers, now in public domain) on pages: (2, 3, 40, 106, 117, 199);
Tim Kirk: (94)

Library of Congress Control Number: 2012938117

Scripture references taken from J.B. Phillips, "The New Testament in Modern English," 1962 edition by Harper Collins.

Printed in the United States of America

2 3 4 5 6 7 8 9 10 Printing/Year 16 15 14 13

for

MAX MILLER

And on the eighth day, God created a few people
with a swinging door between their left and right brain.
My friend Maxwell John Miller's door has been known
to get stuck in the open position *f-f-f-frequently.*

CONTENTS

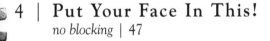

{There will be a fifteen-minute intermission}

Please, take your seats for the second act.

If you don't like change you're going to like irrelevance even less.

General Eric Shinseki,
Former Chief of Staff,
United States Army

I LOVE THE SMELL OF FELT PENS IN THE MORNING!

Nobody knows how to brainstorm anymore. Most corporate brainstorming isn't brainstorming. Sorry, not even close. Usually what's going on is playful arguing with snacks on the table. More than three decades of working in and around immensely creative organizations has demonstrated this to me time and again. If you actually had been brainstorming you would have required fewer follow-up meetings to discuss, "What happened to all those great ideas we came up with?"

If you actually had been brainstorming, you wouldn't have needed my services as a consultant—at least not in the same way. What likely happened is you didn't finish the work of *Creative Thinking*. You hatched an idea—but didn't create a plan to complete that idea. Or you only hatched a few ideas. I think I know why.

☞ Nobody knows how to BRAINSTORM anymore

It's not your colleagues' fault—or yours. *Nobody* knows how to brainstorm because hardly anybody teaches real-deal, high-octane, change-the-game, and make-your-competition-weep-bitter-tears-style brainstorming.

You know this is true. You learned how to do what you think is *brainstorming* from someone who inherited a broken method. If you actually had been brainstorming, your products would be better—*best in class*, your services would be the envy of your industry, your nonprofit would attract volunteers and new donors by the busload.

"But we spent *two hours* 'kicking around' some really good stuff. That's the way we've always done it. Isn't that brainstorming?"

In a word, no. Real brainstorming does not involve any actual *kicking*. Far too often, "the way we've always done it" is the wrong way: the least productive and the most frustrating. It is certainly not the most powerful way—you can tell that by your mediocre, ordinary, predictable results.

The good news is you and your team can learn powerful brainstorming that works—*every time*. Plus, there's an added benefit. As it turns out, real brainstorming is a kick in the pants to do! Imagine having fun and being productive—all at the same time. Done right, brainstorming produces amazing results because ... **we are smarter than me!**

THIS IS NOT A BOOK ON "HOW TO DESIGN THEME PARKS." But if that's your business, this is your book. HATCH! will show you how to use the high-powered, imaginative brainstorming methods used by Disney Imagineers (theme-park designers) to create, plan, and develop new products, services, marketing strategies, or facilities for any organization. (Even for budgets that fit on a Post-It note.) Time to stop arguing and start creating. Former Disney Imagineer C. McNair Wilson's 7 Agreements of Brainstorming™ will assist any team in designing, creating, changing, and launching any project.

HATCH! does not tell you what to think, but how to create MORE ideas and WILDER ideas quickly. Stop trying to figure out the "right" idea or the "perfect" plan. They don't exist.

Whatever is "next" for your organization, why not make sure it's also BEST?

Ah, love that smell

What's the Big Deal About Creativity?

Our organization isn't really all that creative. We're doing fine.

"Fine? Really?" If I asked you, I'll bet you could tell me the names of the "creative people" in your organization. What if everyone in the company directory was *actively creative* and working to improve and enhance every part of your operation? And what if your entire team knew that you expected them to make a contribution to the ongoing creativity of your brand and the daily life of coworkers? If they knew that you thought their input was significant, because you believed in their creativity, would that make any difference at all? Creativity and a workplace that fosters, encourages, and rewards creativity are all standard operating procedure at the world's most successful organizations.

Who are they? You know. A few are mentioned on the next page. Regularly convened brainstorming sessions will foster a creative working environment and creative organization.

Contribution & Significance

CEOs, directors, managers, and even VPs, take heart. True brainstorming contributes to a workplace in which team members discover their individual value and find *significance*— because they are each making a *contribution* to an enterprise larger than themselves. Any organization will benefit from that kind of heightened, authentic, self-confidence.

People working at the top of their intelligence will affect the bottom line.

When people see their coworkers jumping in with creative thinking—and enthusiasm—they will start believing in each other more and more. In such an environment they will begin bouncing ideas off of each other on a regular basis (no kicking required). Soon, brainstorming spills into the halls and tumbles into every office, cubicle, conference, and break room. You will discover actual brainstorming popping up in conversation at local cafés and coffee lounges. Even in casual, after-work gatherings. *That's* a happy hour.

Who Knew?

Does anyone really know how to do brainstorming that works?

Nissan Design knows. It's how they developed a parking garage full of hot cars (and other award-winning products) at their industry-leading design centers in La Jolla, California, and Farmington Hills, Michigan.

Apple Computer knows. That's why they stamp the words *Designed by Apple in California* on a line of iconic consumer devices that streams from the first-generation iPod to the miraculous Macintosh Operating System to the powerful MacBook Pro, iPhone, and the blazingly fast and elegant iPad. And you can be certain they're still creating at Apple HQ in Cupertino.

And ...

For ten years I worked at another outfit that knows real brainstorming—where creative thinking is like playing great jazz. They go by the name of their founder, Disney, and they create the way most people breathe. I know because I was a Disney Imagineer, and later a consultant for several more years with all Disney divisions. Disney Imagineering is where all new Disney theme parks and resorts are dreamt, doodled, designed, developed, delineated, and dispatched. I was fortunate to be part of concept and design teams that hatched a handful of new Disney theme parks, two resort entertainment complexes, a pair of highly themed water parks, the interior theming for a major Disney hotel, and more new attractions than you can shake an E Ticket* at. This mental midwifery was at once challenging, frustrating, daunting, and endlessly rewarding. I always say thinking up theme parks is:

"The hardest fun I've ever done."

*E TICKET was for the big rides in Disney parks—and most **E**xpensive to create. From 1955, Disneyland and Walt Disney World's Magic Kingdom (1971) guests received ticket books with A to E "coupons." The biggest, newest, most popular attractions—Pirates, Matterhorn, etc.—were "E Tickets." An "A" ticket got you a ride down Main Street in a horse-drawn streetcar. More tickets could be purchased as needed. Many California families have a few A, B, and C tickets in a drawer somewhere, but few unused E tickets exist, anywhere. Some thirty years after their demise (1982) you still hear **E Ticket** in pop songs, speeches, and conversation to mean the BEST. "It's an E Ticket." Astronaut Sally Ride (first American woman in space, in 1983) on her first trip on the space shuttle, Challenger, said, "This is definitely an E Ticket!"

§

Early in my time at Imagineering, they noticed that when I put together a team to think up a new theme park or attraction, we got to lots of ideas, big ideas, and we got there quickly—all with brainstorming.

My brainstorming techniques were assembled by Max Miller and me beginning during our pre-Imagineering years at SAK Theatre. We stirred in a few secrets from our background in theatre (especially improv and storytelling). I had been reading and hearing about Walt Disney's methods since I was a young boy—and using them all along for school and church projects. Once I was at Imagineering I gained insights from my many conversations with Disney long-timers. Along the way I folded newly devised exercises we developed to keep things moving positively and productively with the wildly creative and playful minds at Imagineering. Soon, Disney University came knocking and I began teaching my brainstorming methods to Disney management in all divisions—*even legal.*

Please, I am not saying I invented brainstorming. Far from it. I just encouraged my teams to draw on their childhood playfulness and not their adult "who's-the-smartest-person-in-the-room-ness." I encouraged them to return to brainstorming the way Walt and his Dinosaurs of design did in the first golden age of Disney—from Snow White (1937) to Disney World (1971). I also taught my teams the brainstorming methods I found to be the most effective (productive and enjoyable) during a decade with my SAK Theatre Co. prior to joining Disney as a full-time Imagineer.

At SAK and Imagineering, we weren't just playing around to amuse ourselves; we were creating places and events for our *guests* to pay-to-play. Behind all those remarkable theme parks stands a big, fat, media conglomerate that is in business to make a profit (and shareholders who hold them to it). If Disney doesn't watch the bottom line, the bottom drops out and there are no more pirates to "yo ho" in the Magic Kingdom—or on the big screen.

> ✍ **aSECRETagenda** At the heart of my teaching this brainstorming process is a desire to form teams of individuals, while always valuing, respecting, and taking full advantage of each person's creative spirit and individuality. Disney management liked that bonus benefit that I was assisting individuals in my other presentation, **Recapturing Your Creative Spirit**®. I was invited to add that additional presentation to my Disney University classes. I continued to consult and facilitate brainstorming sessions throughout the Disney organization for many years after I moved on from Disney Imagineering into private consulting.

That may work at Disney—BUT I'm not creative!

It won't surprise me if you think you're not creative enough to brainstorm. As energized as the entire Disney organization was, a surprising number of management mice in my Disney U workshops said, "I can't do this. I'm not creative."

I'll tell *you* what I told *them*: "You're wrong."

I am convinced that everyone is born with a built-in creative spirit. I believe creative thinking is the "Maker's Mark"—the image of our Creator. It is what compels every child on earth to sing, dance, draw, paint, make up stories, and raid closets for old hats, big coats, fancy scarves, and ugly neckties. It is that same Creator spirit that finds you driving home down a street you have never driven before, just to see what's there. We call it a *shortcut*, even when it's not a bit shorter. It is your factory-installed creative spirit at work when you rearrange furniture in your office or family room to function *more* effectively, or when you just try something different to get a fresh perspective: Your desk facing the *window* not the *door*. All those are expressions of your creative spirit. You use it *every day*.

Not only does the corporate world brainstorm poorly, we rarely do it at all. We have accepted the lie that brainstorming can only be done by "creatives"—whatever *that* is. Thus, *most people* don't do it at all. "Creativity? Not *this* department. That's on the first floor, in the back corner."

Even when everything is "fine" I say *brainstorm*, HATCH! That old saying, "If it ain't broke, don't fix it," is for people who are satisfied with life, work, and business as usual. Many of my clients bring me in and say, "We're doing real good. Nothing's broken. What are we missing?"

To which I say, "Let's brainstorm to see how we might make what's already good, astonishing, fantastic."

I believe in brainstorming even in the best of times. If it's worth doing (your business), it is worth doing well. This is not about moving from "good-to-great" but *beyond* great. Successful organizations are constantly asking, "What's next?"

Anyone can brainstorm—even you! No matter what product you want to invent or improve, what service you need to make superior to your competition, what ministry endeavor you want to enrich, the keys to brainstorming in this book will work for you. I guarantee it. Since leaving Disney Imagineering, I have taught this process and used it successfully with everyone from junior-high kids to attorneys, NASA engineers, educators, accountants, restauranteurs, not-for-profits, major film studios, ministry professionals, and in facilities so Top Secret, I had to have an escort to get to the men's room—*really*. This stuff works every time—even in countries beyond North America. I keep felt pens and my Creative Thinking hat permanently packed in my suitcase.

Can you recommend a good book on brainstorming?

People have been asking me this for years. I've always squinted, scratched my head, and said, "Um … not really." Eventually it occurred to me that if I couldn't recommend such a book, I should write it.

HATCH! (*fanfare*) is the quest for the huge, the best, the impossible, the never-before-on-this-planet, in businesses and nonprofits, small and large, local, multi-national … and even families. What you hold in your hands, my friend, is a straight-forward, practical "Playbook for Productivity"—a field guide to creativity as a team effort. I have used the techniques in this book at Disney and with a menagerie of clients with whom I have conferred, coached, coaxed, and cajoled in my pre-and post-mouse years. You will even learn how to make a reality of ideas you can't possibly afford. ("But we have such big ideas and such a tiny budget." *Great!*)

`Creativity:` `It's not` `just for the` `"creative"` `anymore.` I'm asking you to tap into your own original, playful, creative spirit. I'm not asking you to act like a big kid—more like a kid with some miles on your dials; a kid with lots of lessons learned, stories to tell, travels taken, trials, errors, loves, and loves lost—dreams dreamt and dashed. When it comes to creating new value, I want you to be an experienced child, a *professional third grader*. The question is not, "Do you have an imagination?" (Everyone does!) The question is, "Do you use your imagination, your natural sense of wonder and curiosity, to make a difference?" Your sense of wonder is one of the best tools you have: *Wonder what it would be like if we …*

DOODLES, IMAGINATION, DAYDREAMS

When I first arrived at Walt Disney Imagineering, I was surprised to find that even there, what they called brainstorming, often *wasn't*. Instead there were playful, non-linear, daylong chat fests, with endless snacks. It was more like "creative dodge ball." The objective in these pages is to assist you to learn a more positive and infinitely more productive way to brainstorm. I call it, simply: **The 7 Agreements of Brainstorming**. This can spark productivity and expand communications throughout your organization—not just in brainstorming.

Don't get me wrong. From day one, Imagineering was the most creatively alive place I have ever worked. The talent pool was overflowing! When there weren't enough ideas we would generate another wall-full. *"Let's fill that wall before lunch."* Then (starting with the smallest wall) we'd think, chatter, and dream 'til the Chinese chicken salad arrived. After lunch, a bigger wall.

The difference is, at Imagineering we were given lots of time to dream. That allowed for our friendly "brainstorming brawls" to erupt, die down, and gurgle along toward an eventual answer. Given enough time, we knew we could come up with a critical mass of ideas, sort through our pile to assemble a solution.

I suspect you seldom have the luxury of time. Chances are you need to land on the best ideas your team can dream up in one morning or a few days (max)—and start implementing them yesterday. If you're lucky, maybe you can work on generating ideas Thursday and Friday and take the weekend to ruminate on them before you have to begin making them a reality come Monday.

Whatever your time frame, I am confident **The 7 Agreements of Brainstorming** will accelerate what you need to accomplish—and you will *enjoy doing it*. Who could demand more than that?

⑨ **YourSHOWofSHOWS** The indefatigable comic actor Sid Caesar pioneered television sketch comedy in the 1950s. He performed ninety minutes LIVE every Saturday night on *Your Show of Shows*. Network "suits" demanded Sid & Co. submit scripts by Thursday. Scripts were rarely ready. The suits pushed. Sid shot back, saying, "Do you want it Thursday or do you want it good?" In brainstorming, I want your team's work to be "good" rather than "Thursday." With the creative thinking tools in *HATCH* I believe you can be both **good** and **Thursday**.

Stop Arguing and Start Creating!

My recipe for creative problem solving—**The 7 Agreements of Brainstorming**—is designed first to create hundreds, even thousands of ideas, quickly, playfully, and without the impediment of constant analysis, needless arguing, executive decree, and judgment by others (and you). In the initial stages, no idea will be criticized or rejected (there will be a time for Critical Thinking, later—*Agreement No. 7*.) And no third-graders will be harmed in this process.

Powerful brainstorming teams really do "play well with others." That requires some ground rules, a set of clear and doable *agreements*. If you use all seven agreements in **The**

7 Agreements of Brainstorming you will find that your brainstorming becomes a high-octane, turbocharged creative vehicle. (If you use only two or three agreements, your creative engine might start, but it will never fire on all cylinders.)

These **7** (simple) **Agreements** will help your team dream up more ideas than you can implement—and then assist your team in mining that mountain of dreams to craft the "best ideas" (solution) into a great product, experience, or service.

If your team will agree to play by these seven rules, I believe you will set a new standard of productivity and teamwork for your organization.

WARNING: Once your team embraces this process, it is likely to spill out of the brainstorming "sandbox," and tumble down the halls into every area of your organization until it becomes the way you work together and communicate every day.

(Cure for the common cold sold separately.)

Onward & upward,

C McNair

C. McNair Wilson
In a café somewhere, writing and doodling the next books.
(*There will be three books in this series. One book has "Gravy" in the title.*)

**Grab your matches
and felt pens ...**

Hell, there are
no rules here,
we're actually trying
to accomplish
something.

Thomas A. Edison

START A FIRE
[hey, Max, you Boy Scouts were right all along.]

My longtime friend and Disney co-conspirator, Maxwell J. Miller, served on the national board of Boy Scouts of America. He still wears his Eagle scout uniform—on special occasions (days ending in "y" and the appearance of the moon). The Boy Scout motto is a good one for nearly all of life: *Be Prepared.* The First **Agreement of Brainstorming** echoes this truism. Like every good Boy Scout worth his merit sash, always have waterproof matches on hand to *start a fire* in your organization.

Here's what that means in practice: Before you convene any creative meeting (all meetings can include creativity), inform everyone (not just participants) of the objective of your session. The goal is to get *everyone* ruminating in advance on the same *target topic.* Especially encourage folks not on the "cc" list to pass their ideas along before, during, and after the creative team gets to work. (I'll address team makeup, later.)

> **"The hardest thing about getting started is getting started."**
>
> **Guy Kawasaki**
> *The Art of the Start*

 ## Agreement No. I: **START A FIRE!**

This is not exactly news, but still worth mentioning: Our psychological wiring is not identical from person to person. Swiss analytical psychologist Carl Jung proposed that everyone tends toward being either an *introvert* or an *extrovert.* Introverts, Jung observed, take their energy from their inner life and ideally work better alone. Extroverts, however, are energized by interacting with others, engaged by exterior stimulus. As I write this, I am sitting in César Cafe in Berkley, California, sipping Earl Grey tea, listening to traditional jazz, people-watching, and oh, yeah, writing a book. I am an extrovert off the chart. (In standardized testing, my *extrovert* score usually appears on the chart of the person two rows ahead of me.)

Extroverts can, at a moment's notice, pop off ideas with no advance preparation. Our introvert friends—equally smart and inventive—deliver their best work with a little lead time to throw another shovel of coal on their inner fire. They are not slow or less facile; they are just differently engaged. I have seen as many grand ideas from properly prepared introverts as from their more rambunctious extrovert friends.

Start a Fire and you will get everyone thinking and talking about what you want them focused on—with the added benefit of letting the team know you believe everyone's ideas are valuable (not just the loud ones). This makes for a creativity-friendly work place.

> ♫ **BUILDING JAZZ** When we were creating **Pleasure Island,** the nighttime entertainment district for Walt Disney World's "Downtown Disney," there were initially six or eight of us on the concept team (out of several hundred Disney Imagineers). Six or eight were plenty at the beginning because we were stopped frequently in the halls by any number of other Imagineers who wanted to say, *Will there be jazz? There'd better be seafood. Hope there's country-western.* In this way hundreds of people stoked the fires of creativity on a project that required the focus of fewer than ten *thinker-uppers.*

Telling *everyone—from reception desk to loading dock*—the target topic in advance generates a buzz in the building, an infectious enthusiasm, for the project. It creates *agreement* and focus before brainstorming work begins.

In an odd way, it begins the work. When you *Start a Fire*, everyone arrives prepared, pointed in one direction. (If you don't know the psychological tendency of each member of your team, the Myers-Briggs personality profile is an accessible survey for discovering this and other traits affecting attitude and decision-making. Your HR folks can assist with this.) Some folks—introverts—need time to think *before* they jump into a brainstorming session. Given time to process their own ideas in advance, they will be fully participatory.

Got a Match?

How do you *start a fire?* An email blast or an insert in pay envelopes works well—I've done this at several companies. (Keep it short, direct, and pithy so folks will read it.) Consider tent cards on tables in break rooms and employee eatery. Be direct where directness serves your ends; be provocative where a little suspense seems in order. One great way to *start a fire* is by hanging small posters around the office. Something like these mini posters to kindle a few sparks… (See, top of next page.)

Taking my own advice, I hereby advise you, my reader, of my intention to work with you on planning the long-overdue *Invasion of Canada!* We'll use the exercise of creating our invasion to focus our thinking in learning the *7 Agreements of Brainstorming.*

For the record, it is only fair that we invade Canada, since they own more of the United States than almost any other country. But that's not why we're going there. The Invasion of Canada is an all-out, full-frontal launch of your organization across the international border into the hamlets, towns, and territories of our northern neighbor. (To

**THE INVASION
BEGINS SOON!**

**WHEN THE INVASION COMES,
ON WHOSE SIDE WILL YOU BE?**

**WE'RE HEADED NORTH,
ARE YOU COMING?**

**HAVE YOU
ENLISTED
YET?**

my Canadian readers: You may instead plan an invasion of Iceland or Vermont—we're not really making good use of it.)

Together, we will brainstorm a product launch and marketing campaign ... some of it in *French(!)* Buckle your seat belts; this is going to be a three looper with a 300-foot vertical drop and a twist at the end!

Time Passes : A few days ... maybe a week

You've started a fire by informing your entire staff of your plans for the Invasion of Canada. Your creative team gathers for the first session. Because you've *started a fire*, your first creative meeting begins with ideas in everyone's mind, on everyone's lips, and echoing through the halls. Everyone—introvert and extrovert alike—arrives ready to play. (In fairness, this may not happen the *very* first time you do it because people may still be hesitant from previous experiences they've had with brainstorming that wasn't really open brainstorming. Be persistent; they'll come around once they understand that from now on brainstorming means business.)

To begin your first brainstorming session, clearly define the single, focused target topic—*Invasion of Canada*—and write it at the top of a big blank pad—or a long horizontal stretch of butcher paper taped to the wall. Be certain everyone on the team understands the target. At the beginning we are imagining what we *might* do, but not necessarily *how* to accomplish every detail of our Invasion of Canada. The target topic focuses the creative energy of the entire team.

Make the early stages of Creative Thinking as easy as possible. Writing everything on big pads, on sturdy easels (*four* legs, not three!), allows everyone to see every idea, thought, whim, notion ... at all times. As each page fills up, tear it off and post it on the wall. When new team members are added, they will step into a place and be surrounded with hundreds of ideas to jump-start their thinking.

It is my experience over decades of this work that laptops—and now iPads, smartphones—are far more of a distraction to creative thinking than they are an aid. You will also see later the power of visual note taking—*The Doodle Factor*. Surfing the net can become an endless rabbit hole that you should fall down *later*.

I understand some plans are and must remain secret until they are launched. When that's the case, even if you can't tell *everyone*, you can still start a fire with your project team and other support staff. The more who can know, the more who will pitch in with their own creative thinking. *More* is a good thing.

Blue Sky Thinking

The one *exception* to brainstorming a single, focused topic as the answer to a particular project is a "blue sky" session that explores big, *What If?* questions for your organization. Once you learn to brainstorm effectively in a team setting, gather your staff occasionally to toss around ideas on *any* subject you like—no boundaries, no focus, no target. When your staff becomes convinced that new ideas are accepted and encouraged, they will pay more acute attention to customer feedback and other issues on a daily basis. They will also become more observant of competitors and related businesses. In a blue sky session we ask, "What's anybody been thinking about?" or, my favorite question, "What have we never done here before?"

DISNEYLAND PARKING NEXT RIGHT ...MAYBE

TWO CIRCLES CHANGED EVERYTHING You might not have met **Disneyland's** newest neighbor. Now a new theme park sits at the front door of Walt's original park in Anaheim, California. I know exactly how Disney's California Adventure ® sprang to life—I was there when it began. For more than forty years the site was a 100-acre parking lot—before that, orange groves. The theme park that sits there now was not the singular brainchild of one very clever person dreaming alone in a corner garret. It was hatched from thousands of little ideas, over months of daylong brainstorming sessions at Imagineering. The ideas that came to define **Disney's California Adventure** ® were not the first ideas we had—or the third. Not even close.

There were just eight of us in the room when Disney CEO Michael Eisner drew two big circles, badly. Pointing to the bottom circle, he said, "If I gave you these one hundred acres of asphalt in front of Disneyland (*a.k.a. the Disneyland parking lot*) what would you do with it?"

"Another theme park?" Somebody asked.

"I don't know."

"But where will everyone park?" Someone had inadvertently invited a Type A to a creative meeting.

"Don't think about that," Michael said. "Give me a reason to move all those cars."

"So it can be anything?"

"You tell me."

We looked at each other with the silly grins of children being asked to redesign their own playground, from scratch.

"You can go now, Mr. Eisner. Thanks for stopping byyyyyeeee."

(Michael was called Mr. Eisner only in jest and this was *jest* such an occasion.)

So for six hours a day, three or four days a week, for *months*, we scribbled, scratched, and imagined brand new worlds to become the new neighbor to Walt Disney's Land.

When he launched us on our creative journey, Michael Eisner modeled one of the great Creative Thinking imperatives: *Ask a big question!* There was plenty of room for our big dreams to run wild on this project—one hundred acres—bigger than Disneyland itself.

We dreamed up more than just one answer to the original question: *What would you put in the parking lot?* We could have built three or four new parks with all our ideas. Only one would fit.

Michael's query about the Disneyland parking lot was a *blue sky* exercise—virtually nothing was out of bounds. The target was expanding the Disneyland guest experience by remodeling a big asphalt spot on the map of Southern California. Remember, Michael would not even narrow our thinking to *theme park*.

He *started a fire* that day, a big one. (Michael had big matches.) Imagineering is a terrible place to try to keep a secret. Word spread quickly, and soon everyone weighed in with their ideas—from support staff and security folks to accounts receivable and even our remarkable café staff.

Convene periodic *blue sky* sessions to fan the flames of your organization's creative fire. Toss everyone into the think tank during lunch (Brown Bag Brainstorming) once a month and see what comes of frequent free thinking! The fewer the boundaries, the more freely their creativity will soar.

℘ Working Definitions:

imagination noun The faculty, ability, or action of forming new ideas, images, or concepts of external objects, places, and procedures not present. In other words, the ability of your mind to think of anything that does not exist at the moment. And, the ability to think of solutions to problems or tasks, that have not been tried, tested, or constructed.

creativity noun To make the new or rearrange the old to appear new through the use of imagination, inspiration, using any skills necessary to accomplish the task.

That's the point: letting imaginations soar. One of my *least* favorite sayings is, *"The sky's the limit."* Think about that. The phrase suggests that even when we're thinking big, there is still a limit—*the sky*. I say,

"The Sky is NOT the limit."

Just ask Neil Armstrong, "Buzz" Aldrin, Pete Conrad, Alan Bean, Alan Shepard, Edgar Mitchell, James Irwin, David Scott, Charles Duke, John Young, Harrison Schmitt, and Gene Cernan.

In *McNair's Fourth Collegiate Drop-outs Dictionary* "creativity" is always (and only) a verb—even when you're just sittin' around thinking, all by yourself, with Mahler's *Eighth Symphony* playing. (The last movement.) Notice that the word "art" doesn't appear in either the definition of *imagination* or *creativity*.

When dealing in imagination and creativity, beware the *fiduciary hit squads*: budgetary boogeymen with cloying concerns, technical feasibility studies, time constraints, flow charts, and a survey or study proving us wrong, *statistically!* These are just a few of the assassins of dreams and curiosity. There will be ample time to get practical—*later*. For now, concentrate on that *fire* you've started. In short order, everyone will add a log, a fistful of twigs, or an old phone book. Brainstorming is not as simple as *"Got any good ideas? Fine, we'll use* that one. *Thanks for coming. Drive safely."* If it were, this book would be unnecessary. There's a bit more to it. Let's …

GETGOINGGOINGGOINGGOINGGOINGGOINGGOING

RECAP

👉 Agreement No. 1: START A FIRE!

- **Launch a rumor.** Get the word out, to everyone. Notify all participants of the "target topic" in advance. Giving introverts time to start thinking won't hurt extroverts a bit.
- **Distribute The 7 Agreements of Brainstorming** (the book to first-timers, a summary to those who have read it) for everyone to bone up on brainstorming.
- **"Target Topic."** Write the project topic ("Canada Invasion") at the top of a big blank pad and clarify the project. Every subsequent sheet should have a title at the top, target topic, subtopic …
- **No boundaries brain bouncing.** From time to time, convene a **"blue sky"** session to see what you might dream up on ANY topic. This also maintains the spirit of your organization being "open to new ideas" on anything.

Always carry: wood, water and fire and you'll be safe from monsters.

"We sorta do that now. Sorta."

CEO of a very big company
in response to my question about
their current creative process

SEPARATE TWO EGGS

[*the first reason most brainstorming fails*]

The biggest sin in nearly every brainstorming session is failing to distinguish and clearly separate *Creative Thinking* and *Critical Thinking*. These are the two, *separate* yet vital activities of every brainstorming process. Brainstorming, to succeed, requires that these two fragile, equally important components be kept far away from each other—because each is capable of destroying the other.

☞ Agreement No. 2: **THINK DISTINCTIVELY**

Start your brainstorming—Canada Invasion—by separating *Creative Thinking* and *Critical Thinking*. Both must be done, but they must be done separately if anything of lasting value will be accomplished. **Creative Thinking** is idea-generating, imagining, wondering out loud, dreaming, "what-iffing."

The decidedly different activity of **Critical Thinking** is not so much thinking negatively as it is thinking with analysis, focus, intentionality, and purpose. It is even possible, I believe, to practice a form of positive, proactive, and creatively expansive *Critical Thinking*. (More, later. *Critical Thinking* is Agreement No. 7.)

There are a hundred excuses for the *sin* of scrambling Creative and Critical Thinking together as one process in most brainstorming sessions. At the top of the excuse hit parade are:

• *We don't have much time.*
• *Thinking and evaluating simultaneously gets rid of bad ideas as we go along.*
• *We're all friends, what's the big deal?*
• *This is how we've always done it.*
• *We're just gonna toss out a few quick ideas, pick one, and go for it.*

When I describe a more powerful method, corporate clients often say, "Well, we *sorta* do that now."

"That's why," I say, "you *sorta* have *sorta* good ideas and are *sorta* doing okay, but *sorta* need a new way of working. *Sorta.*"

"We sure do," someone moans from the back of the room.

You will have made huge strides toward powerful Creative Thinking once your team embraces and *agrees to* this important distinction: Creative and Critical Thinking are not part of the same activity and do not, cannot, *must not* occur simultaneously. It doesn't work. They cannot occupy the same space. They are the beginning and end of the process whether it is five minutes or five months. Folding them together means doing neither activity effectively. And it is not brainstorming.

> O, that way
> madness lies; let
> me shun that!
>
> King Lear, Act III, sc. iv
> William Shakespeare

You cannot be *fully, actively creative* if you are simultaneously *thinking* critically.

"Yes, I can, McNair."

I know you *think* you can, Sparky, but the results show it ain't working.

If you bounce directly from idea to critique, what you are actually doing is very negative thinking about every little *piece* of an idea that comes to mind. Let each idea or thought get out there and be considered.

It is vital that you learn to postpone judgment, evaluation, and analysis until you and your team get everything out of your head and up on the wall. You are hatching a plan. Every chicken, eventually, leaves the egg. During Creative Thinking you are offering thought fragments, whims, notions, doodles, bits, and pieces. Your organization's Canada launch (or Vermont invasion) will be an amalgam of *hundreds* of smaller ideas, melded to form a whole concept. The final concept never arrives fully formed. *Never.*

Before you have critical or analytical thoughts, create for a while. Don't think, *play.* Decide nothing, other than to continue playing with ideas. The key to vigorous Creative Thinking is to:

Learn Not To Care

That is to say, get to a point where you *learn not to care* if your ideas make sense, are possible, or if they fit into the project budget. You will care about all that later. This is true for all the ideas that flash through your *mind* during Creative Thinking.

Don't deliberate, *divulge.*

Don't analyze, *add.*

Don't decide, *confide.*

Don't edit, *say it.*

A studio vice president, taking my Disney University brainstorming class, said, "So, during Creative Thinking we shouldn't overthink."

"Don't try to figure it out," I said. "Maybe don't actually think at all."

"I can do that." He smirked.

"You're great at not thinking." His friend chimed in.

Say it all—*whatever* comes to mind.

Creative Thinking is an active, participatory, forward-moving force of nature. Say everything that comes to mind—quickly! (Before *you* have a chance to critically evaluate even your *own* ideas.)

You cannot possibly know when a tiny, fleeting thought will be just the spark to ignite a bonfire of creativity in other team members.

For more than three decades I have worked with Youth Specialties, a San Diego-based organization that creates conventions and truckloads of other creative resources for ministry professionals and volunteers who work with teenagers. Among a monstrously inventive staff, two inmates at YS stand out like a car alarm in a convent: co-founder Mike Yaconelli (RIP) and Tic Long, the majordomo of YS conventions. Once "Yac" and Tic know the target topic, they're off like Olympic-caliber daydreamers. Are they the brightest guys in the room? Who knows? Their secret weapon is—are you sitting down—*they don't care*. They don't care if their ideas will work, if anybody likes their ideas, or even if they make sense. They don't even care if they're right (gasp). All those things will be sorted out and attended to *later*. Learning not to care is learning not to take the process personally.

Is This Going to Take Long? (I have a 2:00 Skype with Altoona)

The whole process—all **7 Agreements of Brainstorming**—can take as little as a few minutes, depending on the plan you need to HATCH!

Camp director gathers his team after breakfast. "Tonight's campfire talk is on hiking safety and basic survival. We've got a *Survivor* skit when we'll vote a counselor 'off the bleachers.' We need some fun survival and hiking songs. Go!"

Staff members rifle off dozens of suggestions out loud: boom, boom, boom, boom, boom ...

"Great." Then they select. "How about bam, bam, bam ... those three and bam at the end of campfire."

Boom, boom, boom, boom, boom is Creative Thinking.

"*Bam, bam, bam*" is Critical Thinking. Create first, then select and decide. All this happens while standing in a quickly assembled huddle at the back of the dining hall. Next they're off to judge cabin cleanup.

Same scene. This time each song suggestion, *boom*, is met with a reason why that's *not* a good choice, "*Clang!*" How much gets done when every idea—big or small—is met with the equally powerful punch of a clanging critic? Using the idea/immediate critique mode, very little creating happens. Actually almost none. No wonder that version of brainstorming has always been so unproductive.

Far too many brainstorming sessions become "**Idea Smack Down VIII: This Time It's Personal.**" Once people get shot down a couple of times, they (wisely) stop exposing themselves to what feels very much like enemy fire. They stop thinking, they shut up, they have left the building—emotionally.

But if every idea gets initially accepted without comment, everyone is more likely to offer anything they can think of and be encouraged to imagine more. Our goal in brainstorming is not judging individual ideas. It's selecting, then developing, the ideas that meet our specific goals—or exceed them. Selecting comes later, after we have LOTS of ideas from which to choose.

Whether you have days, weeks, or months to imagine your Canada Invasion (or

In the beginning ... create.

tonight's campfire songs), you'll weaken the processes—and diminish productivity—if you allow *Critical Thinking* in the room during *Creative Thinking*. Stop it, stop it, stop it!

Today: **Canada Invasion.**

Creative Thinking is to: develop, build, arrange, fix, produce, design, write, solve, dream, improve, invent, imagine, choose, discover, rearrange, rekindle, rethink, recall, review ...

renew,
   revive,
      replace,
         revisit,
            restore,
               refresh,
                  reshape.

Stop *overthinking*. Start running off at the heart, soul, mind, and mouth. Begin with a spark and a flame—sounds about right for an invasion. *Shhhh, listen*. Can you hear it? Something cracking open!

> ⑨ **Try this:** What are the first one hundred things that come to mind when you think "Invasion"? Write them all down ... ah, UP for all to see, at all times. (Then one hundred impressions on "Canada.") When you first saw the teaser posters around the office ("The Invasion is coming!") what came to mind? What were people talking about in the coffee room? In the early going, even half-baked ideas are good. Actually, at this point, nothing is baked—or even mixed. You are imagining pieces of a whole, possibilities, ingredients. These are just parts. [Some assembly required—later.]

SCRIBBLING & DOODLING

Write everything down so team members can see it all. (More about this later.) You will be surprised how often your mind—and eyes—will wander around the room, re-reading lists of ideas or scanning doodles from earlier today or last Tuesday. Then, BAM! —a spark, a flash that becomes the catalyst for a new direction. Never think that any idea is too silly, simple, or stupid. Those are all evaluations. To even think an idea is silly means you are already doing Critical Thinking. *Silly* may be precisely what this invasion needs. Certainly Canada could use more silly.

The key in Creative Thinking is to amass MORE ideas than you could possibly use. When you think you have "enough" ideas or even "plenty to pick from," take a break. Then come back and create MORE, and more, and … (more on this, soon).

Let me boil down the Creative Thinking instruction manual to three words: **Think, Say, Write**— or *Doodle* (get it on the wall).

Whatever comes to mind (everything, anything) — **SAY IT**, out loud for all to hear.

Whatever anyone says, **WRITE IT DOWN**—*words or pictures*. A "bad" (simple) doodle is better than a lost idea.

Capture all of it. Post it for all to see.

You are about to HATCH! a plan to invade Canada.

What do y'think?

Recap

Agreement No. 2: TH!NK DISTINCTIVELY

Creative Thinking is always a distinctly different and **separate** activity from **Critical Thinking**—no matter how long you spend HATCHing a plan.

- **Separate Creative Thinking** as a stand-alone activity from Critical Thinking (Agreement No. 7).
- **Start with inventing,** creating, and imagining a big pile of ideas.
- **Say everything that comes to mind.** Hold nothing back.
- **Write it all down** and post everything around the room for everyone to see.
- **Learn not to care** whether any idea will work, make sense, or is affordable—for now.
- **No commentary,** no analysis, critique, or decision-making—*Critical Thinking* comes later. It is a separate, different process from creating.
- **Creative Thinking is messy, loud,** playful, chaotic, non-linear, fun, exhausting, and highly productive. (The hidden secret of a good brainstorming session is that it is also a great team-building activity.)
- **Three words**—It all boils down to: **Think. Say. Write.**

"Makes sense to me that we should Think Creatively before we Think Critically. What are your thoughts, Lou?"

"As you are well aware,
Joseph, I have a
particular proclivity
to criticize. Thus
I shall sit out this
round until we come
to Critical Thinking.
At that point I shall
rejoin the fray with
alacrity and verve!"

"Anyone who wishes to, can play."

Viola Spolin
Director, teacher, author

STOP ARGUING, START CREATING
[*the power of words*]

"What if ... "
Well, maybe, but ...
"Why not ..."
Cause, well, it wouldn't ...
"Maybe we could ..."
N a a a a a a a a a a a h.
"I know!"
I don't think so.
"Nope."
We've been talking for five minutes and don't have even one idea *written down!*
Sound familiar? This is the sound of brainstorming trying to get started—the old, broken way. Like trying to *start a fire* with wet matches.

It's what I call the "train of thought to nowhere." They've taken so many sidetracks, they barely remember the destination they had in mind. This kind of interaction extinguishes any spark of the new, unusual, fresh, lively, untempered, spicy, or shocking. It prevents the unexpected and jettisons the joyful. The *unexpected* is precisely what we hope for when we invade Canada. *Ordinary* is over. Everyone has done *ordinary*. *Ordinary* will not do. Time to *stop arguing and start creating.*

☞ Agreement No. 3: **"YES, AND ..."**

It has been estimated that a child will be told "No" up to *forty thousand* times *before* their first day of kindergarten. That's only twenty-two times a day. The experts are lying; it has to be more than that. My guess is that many a childhood "No" could easily and more valuably have been a "Yes."

A TRUE STORY: A group of children—not a trained actor among them—creates a stage performance after a few basic workshops. For theatre veteran Viola Spolin, observing them playing unselfishly is a revelation. She resolves that children's games can be a basis for exploring the works of theatre. Thus Viola creates "theatre games" that form the foundation for today's popular improvisational theatre. In the opening lines of Spolin's seminal book, *Improvisation for the Theater* (1963), she makes her case directly: "Everyone can act …Everyone can improv …Anyone who wishes to can play."

At the center of these "games" is storytelling. They're just play, yet the improvisational theatre movement Viola Spolin launched has made an immeasurable contribution to the lives of thousands on stage and millions in the audience: And Spolin begat Story Theatre; and Story Theatre begat Second City, and Dudley Riggs, and Saturday Night Live, and *Waiting for Guffman*, SAK Theatre, *Whose Line is it Anyway*, *Mad TV*, and that great little improv club in your town. (If they offer improv classes, take your team.)

In my more than forty years as an actor, director, and playwright, I have participated in and facilitated hundreds of hours of improvisational theatre games. In improv, a make-believe world is created from simple suggestions.

First actor: "Good morning."

Second actor: "Good morning. And how are you?"

No surprises. The second actor builds upon what was *there*—a greeting and time of day, *morning*. One of the immutable ground rules of improv is: *"Yes, and …"*

Yes, and … agrees with what's been "placed on the table," then adds to it. Every action or spoken line conspires to advance the story. Listen, react, add, contribute, build … Yes, and …how 'bout this?

"Good morning."

"**Yes**, it is morning, **and** good morning to you."

During *Creative Thinking*, you have no better friend than the words "YES, AND"—a powerful tool fashioned from two simple words. "Yes, and …" (It came very close to being the title of this book.)

My street theatre company, SAK Theatre, held a dangerous and unique trick at the heart of all our shows at Disney World and elsewhere: We enlisted total strangers, plucked from our audience, and instantly transformed them into Romeo and/or Juliet, or King Arthur, Julius Caesar, Ebenezer Scrooge, etc. We threw our audience-cast members curves, sliders, change-ups, and more than a few spitballs. If they gave back what we asked for, that was good. When they *didn't* do what we suggested or did something completely different, that was *better*. Our task: make *everything* work. "Yes, and" was the glue that held our shows together. There was nothing a guest could say to us that we couldn't agree with and add to for comic effect. SAK Theatre was a mosaic of madness and mayhem bonded by "yes, and"—an indispensable connective tissue.

At the heart of effective, dynamic brainstorming is *agreement*. "Yes, and" serves as that ongoing agreement throughout. This theatrical device creates momentum, maintains forward progress, and, as you will soon see, monitors malcontents.

"Yes, And …" @ Work

Here's how it works: During *Creative Thinking*, *every* response to *any* idea must begin with the words "Yes, and …" spoken aloud at the beginning of any comment. "I've got it!" someone says. "For our Invasion of Canada, I know a guy who collects old Army and Navy stuff just outside of town, in Shokapee. He's got everything—jeeps, tanks, dummy hand grenades, helmets, uniforms. You name it, he's got it."

Idea: *Military surplus.* Write it down. *Everything* spoken gets written down. Everything you think of, is spoken out loud. [**Think, speak, write,** add—*repeat.*]

Idea: "We'll dress in military uniforms."

Response: "Yes, and ...we could make up our own country ... the Grand Duchy of—"

"Yes! *And* ... I want to be a general, with lots of medals, a sash, and a long sword!"

"Yes! And, I know the marching band director at the university. They can march in front of us!"

"Hey, ah, I mean ... Yes, and ... Ugonnalovitstan!"

"Huh? Oh, no—I mean *Yes, and* ... can-you-spell-that, Al?"

"The name of our country: the Grand Duchy of You-gonna-love-it-stan."

"Stan *who?*"

"Didn't you mean *Yes, and* ... *who's* Stan, Letha?"

"*Yes and*, a few in our group are against war." (Dancing on the dangerous edge of the negative abyss of critical thinking.)

"Yes, and, if we do it in an exaggerated farcical way, it would be clearly seen as a stunt, a spoof."

"Of course ... I mean Yes, and ... I knew that. And our troops carry squirt guns, and—"

"*And* ... Super Soakers, and—"

"*Yes, and* ... big banners with our logo on them."

"*Yes, and* ... our logo is on everything: tanks, jeeps, helmets—"

"With a, Doh!—*Yes, and* ... plum-colored helmets, like our logo."

"Yes, and helmets and tanks in PMS 518c!—our official company color."

"Yes, and ... Huh?!"

"*Yes, and* ... shoulder patches. Anywhere there might usually be a military insignia, is our logo."

"*Yes, and* ... the music is a march, but a fun march, like a college fight song."

"Or circus marches, Yes, and circus!"

"Yes, and ..." So it goes. From one simple suggestion, *military surplus,* we have the beginnings of our first concept for the Canada launch. We could stop here. Let's not!

"*Yes, and* ... an aerial strike, simultaneously over Montreal, Toronto, and Vancouver."

"What do we bomb them with? I mean "Yes, and ... what, do we ...?"

"*Yes, and* ... no bombs, *skydivers* with our logo on their parachutes. Fifty of them all at once."

"*Yes, and* ... a *hundred,* and in formation like they did over the Olympic Games in Seoul, Korea."

As grand plans fly around the room—and drop out of the sky—"Yes, and ..." propels the process forward.

Yes.

§ **INNER ACCOUNTANT** Your "inner accountant" is saying, "Do you have any idea what one hundred parachutists, parachuters ... will cost?!" When that occurs, send him out for coffee. (Specify freshly harvested beans, from the eastern slopes of Bolivia, grown with rain water captured in a hand-crafted mug.) Tell him to be back in time for the Critical Thinking portion of the Canada Invasion. Be sure to give your inner accountant the wrong time to be back.

During a daylong workshop with more than one hundred summer camp professionals, I often divided them into groups of five or less. First: "Make a list of all the things you have *never done at your camp.*"

Dead silence holds the room as mind dancing begins. Everyone's eyes roll as they translate the simple question into what they think I really meant. *Hmmm ... never done at camp ...*

"Aim for the impossible!" I add. "Walt Disney was fond of saying, '*It's kind of fun to do the impossible!*'"

(Please notice that I ask *what*, not *how*. "How" comes later.)

Target topic: new, improbable, amazing ideas for your camp.

One table immediately exploded into laughter.

I rush over and ask, "What's up?"

"Howard said his camp doesn't have waterskiing."

"Yes? And ...?" I said.

"Howard's camp doesn't have a lake!"

"Details!" Howard said, "Yes, AND, we'll dig a lake. Most of the camps here have man-made lakes."

My new and creative friend, Howard, heard the actual, question. Everyone else had decided that what I meant to ask was:

"What have we never done at camp ... *that we have facilities for?*

… that we can afford?
… that we know how to do?
… that they'll let us get away with?

Creative Thinking is not linear. It does not progress logically from one idea to the most obvious ideas right next to it. Save your logic for planning and implementing. During Creative Thinking there is no value in phrases like: *How will we do that? Can we afford it?* Or *What does that mean?* Those questions can come later. First … ideas.

For the Canada Invasion consider jump-starting everyone's brain by dividing into teams of just two or three and each create a list of one hundred things your company has *never* used as a marketing tool.

Remember: *Learn Not To Care!*
Abandoned the practical & the affordable!
Start a waterskiing club, *then* dig the lake.

On the Other Hand

We've created an idea for a military invasion of Canada with a comic force from a fictitious country, all from only two words: *military surplus.*

"How about an indoor event?"

"Yes, and … what are you thinking?"

"Don't know. So far every idea is outside. What would an *indoor* launch into Canada look like?

"Yes, and … I prefer inside work."

Opposite is another great Creative Thinking tool. What IS it, what ISN'T it, what have we always done? What have we never been?

"Oh, oh, Yes, and … billboards with our product upside-down to catch people's attention."

"Yes, and, the label right-side-up so they can read it."

"Yes, and *both*—two different billboards."

"Yes, and the tag line is, 'There's another way to look at … (skin care, diet drinks, rental cars …)'"

Noisy, Crazy, Messy

Creative Thinking is neither neat nor organized. It will get messy. Done well— enthusiastically—it can get pretty darn noisy and more than a little crazy. Perfectionists, control freaks, and "high–A" personalities will learn to love the Creative Thinking process for its results. (Take comfort, though, it is not one long noisy event.) But in the early stages, brainstorming looks like constant chaos. It is not. No matter the decibel level, the noise must never be allowed to drown out even the smallest thought or quietest team member. *Every* idea gets written down because it is axiomatic that the *quality* of the ultimate idea is directly related to the *quantity* of early ideas. *Believe it.* (Even if you don't comprehend it now.)

In the process of developing the best products, services, movies, theme parks, sermons, restaurant concepts, lesson plans, novels, video games, and toys, thousands of brilliant creative teams had to HATCH! thousands of great ideas that never got off the brainstorming wall—*never got used.* Why? Because in the creative process better and best ideas beat them out.

When it was determined that a major new attraction was needed for the left side of Disneyland, someone said "log ride." That could easily have been dismissed with, "Every old amusement park has a log ride." But it wasn't dismissed. They wrote it down, got it on the wall, and after lots of "yes, and-ing," it was attached to a mountain of other ideas that became "Splash Mountain." And every day, people in Anaheim, Orlando,

"All good ideas must die (so that great ideas might live)."
Hugh MacLeod, author/cartoonist
Ignore Everybody (book)

and Tokyo wait in long lines for that "*old* log ride" idea.

In Creative Thinking—the *idea* stage—you must let go of your need to "make sense" and the desire to get a quick "answer" or easy "solutions." Learn to just play for a while. You can get going at such a feverish pace during Creative Thinking that you won't be able to stop or notice where you are. Don't try to make sense of it.

Play on!

"Yes, and …" allows shifts more abrupt than switching your cable box from *I Love Lucy* reruns to Jack Bauer saving the world in *24* hours. Since every thought, every idea is written down, you can glance at your long-forgotten lists from yesterday morning's initial burst (posted around the room) and be inspired today at 3:29—or a month from now.

"Yes, and … on Robin's idea for a homecoming parade. Not floats, but a steam train chugging right down Young Street through the heart of Toronto."

"Yes, and … with a sign that reads 'North Pole or Bust!'"

"Young Street?"

"The longest street in North America."

"Yes, and, that's going to be a long parade!"

"Yes, and … how do you know it's the longest street?"

"It's one of the facts I know about Canada."

"What's the other one?"

"It has a total population smaller than California."

"Really?"

"*Yes. And* come to think of it, we shouldn't *invade* Canada, we should annex it. Make it the fifty-first state."

"Yes, and … name it after our product."

"Yes, and … American flags with an extra star."

"Yes, and, instead of a fifty-first star, a tiny, white, Canadian maple leaf."

"Yes, and ... the extra star is *our logo!*"

"YES!"

"AND ...?"

"And nothing. Just ... YES!"

You can see how "Yes, and ..." throws more coal in the furnace, and our train of thought goes wherever our imaginations can take us—laying more tracks as we go. Ch, ch, ch, ch ...

"Yes, and ... throw some more coal on that fire, Bert."

Surely You Jest?

If the question hasn't been rattling around in your brain already, I'll ask it for you. "Do you *really* say '*yes, and*' every time? Doesn't it get monotonous? Yes, and ... yes, and ... yes, and ... blah, blah, blah."

What's monotonous is when every idea is met with immediate criticism, evaluation, or commentary from out of nowhere like an egg tossed from a passing car. Drive-by critics are never helpful. Creative Thinking is not the time for criticism or analysis. "Yes, and ..." thwarts carping commentary. (Carping is a sport in Minnesota.)

Here is an archive of arguments heard f-f-f-frequently in Creative Thinking sessions. Avoid them all:

- **That'll never work.**
- **What's THAT mean?**
- **What, are you nuts?**
- What's that gonna cost?
- **We tried that before.**
- Now THAT'S original ...
- **Not in your lifetime!**
- Double your medication, now.
- **They'll never let us do that.**
- And the golden oldie of criticism: **We've never done it that way before.**

Every one of these phrases, and dozens more you've heard—and *said*—too many times, can ambush the creative process like logs laid across the railroad tracks. The solution: Ch, ch, ch, ch, change your *What's that?* to *What if!* Switch from *What the h - - - ?* to *Why not?!*

Creative Thinking needn't explain, figure out, plan, justify, budget, or even *try* to make sense. Its only function is to make ideas—tons of 'em.

Here are a few non-argumentative alternatives when exploring someone's weird idea.
Say:

Yes, and ... tell me more.

Yes, and ... fascinating. Have you ever seen anything like it?

Yes, and ... what else do you know? Fill us in, please.

Yes, and ... I like where you're headed. Keep talking.

Yes, and ... very interesting. Expand on that ... give us more details.

> ✒ **Try this**: Yes, and, what if instead of a ground invasion of Canada, it's a
> rocket launch? What comes to mind? Outer space. Shuttle flight. Moon
> landing. Or alien invaders from outer space ... or the "lower fifty" as
> our maple leaf northern neighbors call us.

"Yes, and ... a big rocket with a space shuttle lands in downtown Ottawa."

"Where'd *that* come from?"

"Florida. Cape Canaveral."

"Yes, and ... OGLE-TR-56b!"

"Huh? I mean ... Yes, and HUH?!"

"It's the farthest known planet, in the constellation Sagittarius."

"Yes, and ... tell us more. Where's that?"

"Due east of Pittsburgh."

"Yes, *and* ... where'd the idea for a space program for our Canada launch come from?"

"Yes, and ... *you* said it.

"What?"

"Our product launch. What if we do the entire campaign as a space program ..."

"Aah ... I mean, *yes, and* AAAH!"

RECAP

☞ Agreement No. 3: "Yes, and ..."

"Yes, and ..." keeps the creative process moving forward. It is virtually impossible to be negative, critical, disagreeable, or argumentative when you begin each comment with "Yes, and ..." Without these two words, we risk grinding to a halt. At this stage, the project suffers. Productivity bogs down, stops.

There's nothing to be gained at this point in doubting or criticizing—not even playfully. **Don't do it!** (Attitude plays an enormous role in brainstorming.) The only bad ideas are the **unexpressed** ideas we keep in our heads.

The power of **"Yes, and ..."** is as clear as a newly squeegeed window. You say, "Yes," meaning, "I hear all that idea ... AND how about this too?"

- **Learn not to care** (about cost or feasibility of any idea).
- **Think** up. **Speak** up. **Write** it down. Get it up on the wall.
- **Add to anything that is offered.** Build upon every idea.
- **Maintain a free flow of ideas.** Don't stop to "figure it out."
- **No technical or financial details are needed.** Don't analyze.
- **PLAY!** Do not be afraid to be loud, wacky, nonlinear, messy.
- **Develop a propensity for the improbable.**
- **All ideas are accepted** during Creative Thinking.

"Here's the real difference between a conference room and one of your brainstorm shelter deals: In a conference room the waste baskets are full of old notes, doodles, and bits of paper, old magazines. BUT in your standard brainstorm bomb shelter room the waste baskets are empty and everything (Snickers wrappers, doodles, tea bags, maps, post cards) is pinned to the walls. And I mean every THING. Fine by me. I pinned a couple of my own thoughts up there."

Evelyn Preen
Facilities Continuity Associate

PUT YOUR FACE IN THIS!

By now you've thought of a particular person (or two) in your organization who is a notorious analyzer, criticizer, or arguer. Every organization has at least one. (If no one comes to mind, it's *you!*) For such as these, "Yes, and …" will prove difficult. We have tolerated the corrosive effects of these company curmudgeons far too long.

☞ Agreement 4: **NO BLOCKING**

Try this: A large bowl—big enough to accommodate a splendid salad for all—resides in the middle of the table. It is empty. Rather than tossing mixed greens *out* of this bowl for lunch, we'll toss greenbacks *into* it. Whenever someone *blocks* an idea with a negative reaction or criticism, it costs the "blocker" one dollar, cash. (In Canada: toss in a Loonie.) Those who typically contribute a running commentary of negativity will need to start showing up at brainstorming sessions with lots of cash.

Egg Handling

"Remember our military invasion idea?" Amy gets us back on target. "What about the American Revolution? We re-enact George Washington crossing the Delaware, as we launch our *revolutionary* product into Canada."

"Would any Canadian be interested in that?" Fair question from Todd, but it is a critique—even if his intentions are good.

Amy backs down. She feels diminished, unimportant—she has been *blocked*. Wiping Todd's egg from her forehead, she says "It's just an idea."

"Hold on, Todd." Ben says, "You're *blocking*! One dollar, sir, *in* the bowl." Ben nudges Todd playfully.

BLOCKING RULE: Anyone may call Blocking on anyone else, whether you feel blocked by them or believe they are blocking another team member—at any time—during Creative Thinking.

Our brains are highly developed filters designed to differentiate (analyze, assess, evaluate, and even protect us) from the billions of data we receive through our senses. Fully 75 percent of what we learn, know, and take in arrives visually. However, during brainstorming, especially Creative Thinking, we must manually override our brains' default setting to differentiate so we can access, accept, and consider *everything*. Big or tall, bitter or sweet, easy or complex, cheap or expensive ... *all* must be considered during Creative Thinking.

"Wait a minute, Ben." (Watch Todd try to put the egg back in the shell.) "I'm just asking. Asking isn't blocking."

"The way *you* asked Amy, that's blocking," Ben says. "By the way, it will cost you a second dollar for blocking *me* on calling you on blocking."

Amy nods. "Ben's right. Saying, *I'm not blocking* is also blocking."

Cha-ching! (Todd pays $2.)

But, but, but ... what if you really just want to ask a question about someone's idea?

Ask! Curiosity is *not* blocking. But you don't need to understand everything during Creative Thinking. Ideas don't need to make sense. When you think someone is on to something valuable, use our old friend *Agreement No. 3*, "Yes, and ..." Let's have Todd re-ask Amy his question.

"Yes, and ... the American Revolution, colonial army, colorful uniforms. Do you have more ideas on this, Amy?—More is good, right, guys?"

"Right!"

"Can I have my $2 back?"

"Nope."

Before Amy can expand on her whim, Ben is all over it.

"Yes, and ... Washington crossing the, ah, St. Lawrence River ... in a PT boat."

"Yes, and ... a *plum* PT boat."

And so it goes.

Blocking slams the brakes on the playfulness of the proceedings. Hence, we place a *fine* on transgressors.

NO BLOCKING is intended to wean participants from the destructive habit of criticizing and arguing. Even as a facilitator, I have been called for blocking. There must be a cost when we don't *play well with others*. One dollar per grouch seems an appropriate sting.

> "In my wide association in various parts of the world, I have yet to find a man, however great or exalted his station, who did not do better work and put forth greater effort under a spirit of approval than he would ever do under a spirit of criticism."
>
> Charles M. Schwab in Dale Carnegie's *How to Win Friends and Influence People*

I have a favorite letter from the pastor of a large church in the San Francisco Bay area. After coaching their staff and board, I left them to brainstorm, in a retreat setting. A few days later I received this:

§ "You really stimulated us to think 'outside' the box ... and gave us tools for working together in a more harmonious and productive way than we ever have in years. Since your 'No Blocking' rule, and bowl, we've made $250,000 toward new projects."

This was a powerful group. I suspect the blocking pot was bigger than he reported. This dynamic church board and staff was filled with bright and strong individuals. They enjoyed each other and had strong opinions that they now could share through a productive process.

PARENTAL WARNING: If you have children, do not show them this book. If you do, they will plague you for the rest of your life: "You're BLOCKING, Mom! Pay up!" I have received countless email reports that kids love quoting the **7 Agreements of Brainstorming**. You have been warned. (And ... the 7 Agreements can also be used to sort out family issues: overlapping schedules, where to go on vacation, "family night out," and more. Imagine a game the whole family can play: "Decision Making.")

If you do make the mistake of sharing HATCH! and the *7 Agreements of Brainstorming* with your children (a "mistake" I heartily encourage) you'll have to figure an age-appropriate charge for *Blocking*. Maybe twenty-five cents with younger kids. And top blocker gets an extra household chore or an hour less TV or Xbox. Why not brainstorm the appropriate fine and what to do with your family's Blocking bowl cash! (Sponsor a child through Compassion International—www.Compassion.com.)

What's important here is to levy a tariff on criticism during Creative Thinking. Whether with a professional team, volunteers, or a family, if you don't attach a cost to blocking, your brainstorming will soon degenerate to the same old *playful arguing with snacks*—very unproductive.

Dumb ideas get blocked ... right?

But what if someone says something really dumb, or stupid, or ... *wrong?*

The real reason behind *No Blocking*, even more than to prevent slowing the creative process, is that people *do not feel safe* in an environment where constant criticism or even *evaluation* is permitted. Even when they are offered in jest, many people will feel ridiculed or personally attacked—even if that is not the intention. When you boil it down, blocking is a subtle form of emotional abuse.

No one likes that. There should be no room in any workplace for this *anytime*.

Todd may think he's merely inquiring about Amy's revolutionary thinking. But if what Amy hears and *feels* is that Todd doesn't doesn't value *her* or her contribution, Amy will withdraw. And in withdrawing she will be neutralized as a creative force—and no one will have the benefit of her creative contribution.

Every day we have opportunities to empower and encourage people we know and work with—or to diminish their spirit and weaken their confidence. Rule of thumb: *The received message IS the message.* Words are important. The way you say something can be more powerful than your actual words.

"The Medium IS the Message."

Marshal McLuhan,
from his book, *The Medium Is the Message*

"But there must be some ideas that are just plain dumb."

The time to evaluate comes later. Notice I haven't suggested you make categories for: *Dumb* ideas, *Expensive* ideas, *Impossible* ideas, *Really Stupid* ideas, and *What-in-tarnation-are-you-thinking?* ideas.

We are on a quest for the remarkable, unexpected, fantastic, unbelievable, brand-new, and never-heard-anything-like-it plan to invade Canada! But that plan will never emerge if people are afraid of being even a little bit wrong on the way to being amazing. The creativity of your launch will say a lot to prospective new customers about the creativity of your organization. During Creative Thinking, **there is no wrong**—except leaving any idea in your head. That's wrong.

An unshared idea might as well not exist.

We must get past fear of what others will think (or say) about our ideas—NO BLOCKING—and your team will have to answer a new question: "How does your group keep coming up with such great *stuff?*"

> 💲 **HowMuchSelf-EsteemCanOneDollarBuy?** Michael Eisner was with us in many creative sessions at Imagineering. Michael is very imaginative and loved to come "play in the sandbox" (my favorite nickname for Imagineering. It's what Walt Disney's called it.) In the midst of one particularly memorable free-flowing session, Michael offered an "idea" that was so far off the map of Normality that three of us—without saying a word—simultaneously put a dollar in the Blocking Bowl. Half the fear I ever had about what other people think of me dissipated in the next moment when Michael Eisner, CEO of the entire Walt Disney Company, and one of the most powerful media leaders on the planet wailed, "What? What's wrong? It's just an idea! Don't you like my idea, McNair? Come on, guys." Reaching for my money clip, I said, "Michael, you must have lots of little ideas you want to get off your chest. Knock yourself out,"—and placed a $20 bill in the Blocking Bowl. **No Blocking,** like "Yes, and …" works to the degree that everyone **agrees** to use it—creatively and playfully.

Everyone has ideas. The challenge is to access them using a supportive, productive process in a playful environment. Every game has established rules—*agreements*—to assure we all play fair. NO BLOCKING is not meant to be limiting, but liberating. It means anyone can say anything! *Anyone can play.*

Some team members will feel the need to help the group avoid wrong turns. They use a gentler, subtler form of blocking.

Be assured, though: They *are* blocking. These concerned "helpers" have created the need for a codicil, an addendum to No Blocking:

☞ Agreement 4a: **NO WIMPING**

"Can I *share* an observation here?" The "helper" begins. "I enjoy watching you all bounce off each other's ideas. (Key word, *watching*.) But I'm *concerned* that we don't rush into this military theme too quickly. The American Revolution theme has decidedly warlike overtones. *And*, George Washington was a known slave owner.

(*A window bursts open. The wind knocks over a large vase in the corner. It crashes on the floor. A wolf howls in the distance. A cold breeze rushes through the room.*)

"I worry about alienating many potential customers," the Helper continues, "before they even hear what we have to offer. A *big tank*, rolling down the streets. *Really?* Even if we shoot bubbles—it is still a big, mean war machine! I cannot sit idly by without expressing my real concern."

That's *wimping*! Stop it! (Notice that our helper was just *listening* and *sitting idly by*, not adding any ideas.)

Wimping is Blocking with a smarmy, condescending attitude in the guise of "sharing a few *concerns*."

Wimping costs *two dollars*! (Unless your organization permits flogging.)

Like its big brother BLOCKING, Wimping can have only a negative effect on the proceedings and participants. *Wimping* is not as direct as blocking, but it is still criticizing. And it is destructive.

Wimping is gooey. It sticks to everything, slows everything down. Stop it before it gets all over everyone!

"Hey," Al says. "Did anyone write down that great idea about tanks shooting bubbles? Gotta love it!"

Yes, and … How many B's in bubbles?

"Never enough!"

It Only Takes a Spark

That little idea you're holding inside your head because "it won't work" or "nobody will like it" might be just the key that unlocks doors to wonderful new places. Your "little" whim can ignite a fire in the imaginations of the entire team.

Mount Disney: Part IV

Most blocking occurs *in our own minds.* We are each our own worst enemies. Psychologists call this very human trait our "inner critic." (Mine has actually won awards.) Simultaneous to the playful banter during brainstorming, there's another flurry of frenetic conversation:

Nah!

They'd never do it. It wouldn't work.

It will be too expensive.

I can't say that; they'll think I'm an idiot … a bigger idiot than they already think.

All those objections run through *your head.* And through my head. Really. I do it. Everyone does it. **Stop it!**

It is not merely unproductive, it is destructive.

There's an idea running around in your head that just may be the key that unlocks a torrent of imagination from everyone.

My suggesting a hotel *inside* a theme park led to an avalanche of *what-have-we-never-put-in-a-theme-park* thinking that didn't end with a hotel.

The best example of that line of inquiry led to the world's most unusual theme park, Disney's Animal Kingdom at Walt Disney World, Florida. At more than five times the size of Disneyland, California, Animal Kingdom (Florida) ran up against major-league blocking throughout its design and development.

Fortunately, for us all, the person standing at the creative helm was an Imagineer who is darn near impervious to blocking, my friend, the indefatigable Joe Rohde (Roe' dee). Joe not only pushes the boundaries, he regularly shreds envelopes marked "Possible." I was in a few of those Animal Kingdom creative sessions, early on, and I know there was all sorts of trepidation about what would be possible, affordable, and permissible. The team had plenty of chances to talk themselves out of all kinds of great stuff, but they didn't. Instead, Joe & Co. soldiered on, hacking their way through uncharted theme park jungles. In 2006 Joe christened Expedition Everest—the largest theme park attraction on the planet (Rising over two hundred feet—twenty stories!—above the Florida landscape, it is the poster boy for NO WIMPING!).

It would be so tempting, and *too easy,* during your Canada Invasion brainstorming to say that all those military tanks and soldiers are unpopular ideas these days. Well, maybe.

Everyone knows if we have soldiers with giant Super Soakers *people will get wet!* Yup, if that's what we end up doing, they will get wet ... and they'll love it. How else do we explain the fact that in aquatic parks everywhere—like Sea World—the seats in the whale arena that always fill up first are the ones marked "WET ZONE."

"Fire up the bubble tank, Sarge!"

When you block your own ideas, you selfishly prevent others from being inspired by your delight-filled curiosity. This is simply not acceptable. When tempted to wimp out, I imagine my mom, her right hand moving side-to-side (at the wrist) in a slapping motion, up where my head would be, saying:

Put Your FACE in THIS !

That's usually enough to *slap* me out of it. (Which she never did, except playfully and gently.)

The Devil & His Advocates

Inevitably, to avoid being called for Blocking, someone will say, "Let me play Devil's Advocate, okay?"

No! The Devil doesn't need a spokesperson. "Playing Devil's Advocate" is just a not-so-clever way of saying, "I want to disagree." (It also means you are a smarty pants because you think you are the only one in the room who realizes that military equipment as a marketing tool might have a negative connotation. Well, DUH.)

Doesn't anyone remember Richard Branson (powerhouse of creative energy behind his more than four hundred companies, including Virgin Airlines) driving a tank down Broadway, in New York City, to launch his Virgin Cola. He used it to plow through a wall of Coca-Cola cans. So angry, warlike, and creative. That little marketing stunt was on the national news around the world.

If someone on your team wants to play Devil's Advocate during Creative Thinking, tell them, "*That* meeting is in the basement. If you hurry, you can get there before they bolt the door." There is a process for weighing benefits and liabilities of a concept. It's called Critical Thinking—and it comes later. Patience. For now, we create!

(No Such Thing as THEE Idea)

Why do we block our own creative thinking? Fear, of course. *What will people say?* And we are too anxious and impatient about getting the "right" answer, right away. To say the right *thing.* Say it correctly. Say it now. That's a disease we all caught (learned) in school—trying to get it *right*, pass the test.

News flash: In brainstorming, especially during Creative Thinking, there's *no such thing as the right answer.* No wrong answer. The final concept for the Canada Invasion will be assembled from hundreds of thoughts over hours and days of imagining, scribbling, and, most of all, reacting to each other's creative wanderings. It takes a village to have an idiot. But in the village of Brainstorming, everyone gets to be the idiot, the fool, the silly one, the class clown, the genius. We are all kids in the sandbox.

Never once have I heard one big, fully formed, complete idea arrive full-blown in a single comment. Not at Disney, Apple, Chick-fil-A, or Johns-Hopkins Applied Physics Lab. "Not nobody, not nohow."

The only bad idea is the unexpressed idea!

That little mustard seed of an idea running around in your head, looking desperately for a way out, may be the spark, to the match, to the fuse, to the explosion of new ideas that leads to a big concept for your Canada Invasion.

Thee Best Little Idea—Ever

Once upon a time … Walt Disney had a "little idea." He wanted to build a small park across the street from Disney Studios. This was the post-war 1940s. He imagined a general store, barber shop, train station, small lake, steam train, picnic area beneath large shade trees, and a ball field for traveling circuses every autumn and local Little League baseball in the spring. It would also replicate scenes from movies he wanted to make—like a studio backlot.

Walt's early plans included a lake and a country church. That project, called "Walt's Little Park," was to be situated across Riverside Drive from Disney Studios in Burbank on a six-acre parcel. Walt enlisted his top movie production designers and animators to collaborate. Eventually a new site for that little park had to be found to accommodate all their (and Walt's) ideas. All those ideas became Disneyland—one hundred acres, not six—and they're still adding new attractions, more than fifty years after Opening Day, July 17, 1955.

Walt's little idea begat Disneyland in 1955. That ninety-acre* idea spawned a bigger idea, Walt Disney World (WDW) near Orlando, Florida (opened 1971). Today, WDW comprises four theme parks, two dozen hotels, a professional sports complex, three water parks, a city-full of eateries, shops, and entertainment clubs and cinemas (Downtown Disney). Walt Disney World occupies a plot of land that is nearly 30,000 acres (*three hundred times larger* than Disneyland). Walt Disney World is roughly *twice* the size of New York City's Manhattan Island. And there are two Disney theme parks in Paris, two in Japan, two in Anaheim, Hong Kong Disneyland (2005), and in 2015, Shanghai Disneyland.

When Disneyland opened in 1955 the *Wall Street Journal* predicted it would fail. *That's* **Blocking**.

---

*The current size of Disneyland, Anaheim, California—the public area inside the railroad tracks—is approximately ninety acres. By comparison, ONE acre is the width of an American football field by eighty-eight yards long.

RECAP

 # Agreement No. 4: NO BLOCKING

NO WIMPING
(No Kidding)

NO BLOCKING, NO WIMPING. Blocking **adds** nothing. It **creates** nothing. It slows down **everything** and runs the risk of depleting spirits and diminishing enthusiasm. Everyone on the team needs the wit, wisdom, and creativity of everyone else. We inspire and expand on each other's ideas. Torturing every idea with incessant evaluation, analysis, and appraisal damages the process. Blocking reduces and eliminates active participation. At the heart of brainstorming is **full** participation by **every** member of the team.

We did pretty good on the BLOCKING BOWL today. Should we donate all of it to the Salvation Army or we could go to Chick-fil-A for Happy Hour?

- **NO BLOCKING**
  anything or anyone
  during Creative Thinking.
- **Every person**
  and every idea is
  accepted. (Silly ideas
  and stupid questions are
  encouraged.)
- **No evaluating,**
  analyzing, criticizing, deciding, testing, feasibility studies, or budgeting—yet.
- **The only BAD IDEAS are the unexpressed,** unshared ideas we keep in our heads.
- **Anyone can call "blocking"** on anyone, at anytime.
- **Blocking costs one dollar** per block, or equivalent.
- **Denying that you're blocking is also blocking.** Add one dollar.
- **Blocking often occurs in your own head.** Stop it.
- **Wimping is blocking** disguised as concern.
- **Devil's Advocates** need not apply. ("The position has been filled.")

When you have completed this section, put your pencil down and sit quietly.

**"Too much
of a good thing
is wonderful."**

Mae West
Philosopher & Vamp

MORE PIЯATES, PLEASE
[*how to think like Walt Disney*]

The most popular ride in the Magic Kingdom began as a big hole in the ground. It stayed that way for years. But the hole wasn't big enough, so they dug an even bigger hole to hold the boatload of additional ideas they HATCHed. How and why the hole got bigger involves another key agreement to powerful brainstorming. I know the *Hole Story*, and it's a great story if you've got a minute. But first, a word from our sponsor, Agreements, Inc.

☞ Agreement No. 5: **MORE IDEAS**

"The best way to have a good idea is to have a lot of ideas." Those are the words of American scientist, Linus Pauling. Pauling was one of the first to work in *quantum chemistry* so he knew about quantity. During Creative Thinking you can have no better friend than Agreement No. 5: **More Ideas**. The more ideas you generate during Creative Thinking, the more options you will have for building full concepts during Critical Thinking. If you are blocking, arguing, analyzing, or critiquing everything as it is offered, you will have very few ideas left. When it comes time for focusing, selecting, and planning you will be staring at blank paper and empty walls. That's not a marketing plan. Maybe you just need giant billboards in major Canadian cities with a giant Post-it® note that reads. "**Amazing marketing idea here—soon.**"

But if no ideas get blocked during Creative Thinking, *More is more!*

We return now to our regularly scheduled programming: **The Hole Idea.**

Ptuesdays with Pterodactyls

They had been gathering for years when I first joined them. I was still fairly new at Imagineering when Claude Coats* first invited me to be his guest at the legendary and exclusive *Dinosaurs Club*—not a *where*, but a *who*. The *Dinosaurs Club* was composed of retired and current senior Disney animators, Imagineers, and film production designers. For years they'd been meeting every Tuesday for lunch. Most weeks there were eight to ten of them in a big leather booth at one of their favorite haunts. The location was never fancy. Their criteria: hearty food, a full bar, separate checks. Mostly they told war stories and critiqued current movie and theme park developments—especially, but not only, Disney creations. They were brilliant, relentless, and honest critics. They were also more fun to be with than a van full of junior-high kids headed for a theme park. (Trust me, I've done both.)

Attendance was entirely voluntary. There could be as many as forty Dinosaurs gathered when one of the old animators released a new book. At the end of my first Dinosaur lunch, Ken Anderson spoke from the head of the table, where he sat most Tuesdays: "Come back anytime, young man."

I was in my mid-30s when Ken Anderson called me "young man." which made me a mere pup to Ken, who had been the art director for *Snow White and the Seven Dwarfs*—released in 1937. (Almost fifty years before my first Dinosaurs lunch.) From then on, I was an honorary dinosaur every week that I wasn't traveling, for nearly ten years.

> ⑤ **CLAUDE COATS*** was set designer for my favorite Magic Kingdom
> ride, Peter Pan's Flight—also Haunted Mansion, Pirates, ... and many,
> many MORE. He created backgrounds for *Lady and the Tramp, Dumbo,*
> and many other Disney animated classics. It was Claude whom I saw
> on *Walt Disney's Wonderful World of Color,* a TV program showing Walt
> the model for Pirates of the Caribbean, pre-opening. Walt introduced
> Claude as an "Imagineer." That was the first time I heard that word,
> and decided then (at age ten) I wanted to be a Disney Imagineer.
> Twenty-three short years later, I became an Imagineer. My first day
> at Disney, I attended a reception celebrating Claude's first fifty years
> of service. My second office at Imagineering was next to Claude's. One
> day he invited me to lunch with "a few of my friends"—who turned out
> to be the legendary Dinosaurs Club! In the history of Disney and all
> theme park design, my friend, Claude Coats, was a giant. He was also
> 6' 7½" tall. In old photos of Imagineers, he's the tall one.

I learned early on that every tale told at a Dinosaur lunch had more than one version, depending on who *wasn't* there to correct that day's version.

One of my favorite tales came from several viewpoints. I cobbled them all together over my years of listening. It only got better as new episodes were added. It was the story of how Pirates of the Caribbean (the attraction, the ride) first came to be at Disneyland.

An idea had been hatched to build a new themed area, New Orleans Square, between Adventureland and Frontierland. Walt loved history and mandated that amid the shops and restaurants would lurk a lair of pirates. A large room on the New Orleans Square blueprints indicated a walk-through attraction of various scenes, in tableau (like frozen figures in a wax museum) of pirate life (motionless, posed mannequins). A hole was dug on the west side of Disneyland, beyond Adventureland, to commence construction of the New Orleans Square development.

Then ... the phone rang and rang ... and rang. Disney Imagineers were engaged to create major themed attractions for the 1964-65 New York World's Fair. The hole in Disneyland sat empty for months while Walt and his merry 'magineers created and opened the Primeval World Diorama (for Ford Motor Co.), Great Moments with Mr. Lincoln (State of Illinois), Carousel of Progress (General Electric), and It's a Small, Small World (Pepsi-Cola). All were a big hit with fairgoers. Later, New York asked Walt Disney to transform the fair site in 1965 into an East Coast Disneyland. Walt declined. (He was already hard at work designing his "little Florida project.")

Meanwhile, back in Southern California, at WED Enterprises (the original name for Imagineering derived from the initials of its founder, Walter Elias Disney) in Glendale, they unrolled the dusty blueprints for New Orleans Square to commence construction at the big hole they had dug in Disneyland. Having invented Audio-animatronics® for all four New York World's Fair attractions (most famously, Mr. Lincoln) Walt realized they might use this new technology for a pirate or three. But active pirates would need *more* room in which to move.

Walt encouraged designers to revisit all their original brainstorming for *more* ways to activate pirates. The redesigned attraction was far too big for the allotted space. (Today the popular Blue Bayou Restaurant occupies the original Pirates space.) Walt told the Imagineers to ignore the blueprints and show him an attraction filled with hearty (drunk), singing (drunker), pillaging (naughty) pirates, and wench-chasing (non-church-going) buccaneers. Every one of the designers and engineers loved the new expanded attraction. They knew Disneyland guests would, too, but feared everyone would just stand and watch all the piratical goings on and never leave Dubloonland. Moving sidewalks were explored: impractical.

"Boats!" Why not use the boats that carried World's Fair visitors through It's a Small World? Ironically, the Small World boats were based on pirate dinghies from Disney's movie version of Robert Lewis Stevenson's *Treasure Island*—Disney's first live action movie (1950). Instead of the pastels of Small World, they'd paint these boats using a muted pirate pallet. Think of it: large boats filled with families on a salty saunter through a world of pillaging pirates and debauchery—*bring the kids and grandma, too! Haarrr!*

Oops! It seems this building full of boats and pillaging privateers was now too big for any spot inside the park's railroad track perimeter. As my friends the Dinosaurs told it, Walt simply said, "Build it on the other side of the tracks, across from New Orleans Square." (Pirates *do* come from the other side of the tracks.)

"How do boats cross railroad tracks?" (Not *blocking* so much as a quest for a solution.)

"Load 'em up in New Orleans Square." Walt was weaving a tale. "Take them on a quiet flow through the bayou (restaurant). Then ... drop them down a waterfall—*under the tracks*—and into the secret, underground, cavernous world of pirate caves and treasure."

Yo Ho, Yo Ho

They would design and build as big a building as was needed to hold a Caribbean port with a shipload of pirates, blasting canons, caves-full of treasure, a dockside town square, dungeon, wench auction and MORE. Then burn it all down.

"But, but, but, how will we get folks back from the far side of the tracks."

"Bring them back UP the waterfall," Walt said. "Because we can!"

It goes without saying—but I will—that to hold all their piratical ideas they had to "think outside the box." In this case the box was defined by tracks of the Disneyland Railroad. They constructed what was, at the time, Disneyland's largest building by "thinking outside the tracks."

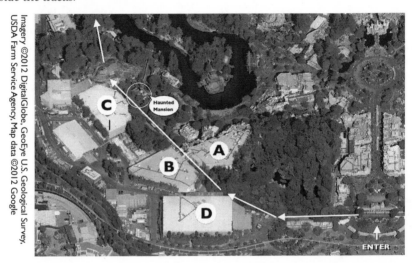

Imagery ©2012 DigitalGlobe, GeoEye U.S. Geological Survey, USDA Farm Service Agency, Map data ©2012 Google

Disneyland: Park Entrance, lower right corner in photo. Main Street USA runs up right side of photo to "Hub" and Sleeping Beauty Castle (upper right). Four large buildings: **A.)** New Orleans Square, shops, Blue Bayou Restaurant, and PIRATES load area; **B.)** PIRATES attraction building; **C.)** HAUNTED MANSION attraction. The actual Haunted Mansion is the smaller building, just right of the Haunted Mansion attraction building inside circle; INDIANA JONES ADVENTURE attraction building **(D.).** Notice, too: the space between New Orleans Square and Pirates building where Disneyland railroad tracks run (arrows). These enormous buildings (B, C, D) are all outside the railroad tracks surrounding the Park. They are hidden from view by, green exterior walls and tall, real trees that serve as camouflage. The only portion of the attraction inside the Haunted Mansion "house" structure is the "expanding (stretching) room" that serves as an elevator to lower guests so they can walk under the railroad tracks and board their "ghost coach" (ride vehicles) in the attraction building **(C.)** Railroad runs through climactic scene in "Splash Mountain" attraction just north of Haunted Mansion. [See full aerial of complete Disneyland Resort, page 73]

To this day, Pirates of the Caribbean remains Disneyland's most popular attraction—on both sides of the tracks and both sides of the continent—and both sides of the Atlantic. All this, born of an unending flow of *more* and *more* ideas (and lots more pirates). And they had to dig another big hole.

It's worth noting that they did something else that marks other creative acts: **Take advantage of the unexpected.** On this occasion, that came in the form of unexpected business generated by the New York World's Fair and break-through technologies, Disney's Audio-animatronics®. Add to that the notion of moving large crowds in big boats (a conveyance system reminiscent of the "Tunnel of Love" in amusement parks of bygone days).

The development of Pirates, the ride, is also the tale of the age-old design question: What-if-our-ideas-are-bigger-than-our-budget? If your ideas are grand enough, it may just be possible, *sometimes*, for the budget to be realigned (increased) to accommodate the BIG idea! (There is a chapter dedicated to big ideas and *tiny* budgets, later in these pages.)

This just in ...

Dateline Huntsville, Texas, Dec. 2011 :: In the final stages of editing this book I received an email from a current client. We have been working for a couple of years on a large, exciting project. They have four hundred-forty acres on a big body of water north of Houston, Texas. They operate two successful camps, but they receive lots of inquiries about a camp for younger kids (ages six to eleven). Virtually no one serves that age group for a "sleep away" camp (apart from a family camp experience). But what if you only went away for half a week? This gives younger kids a camping experience without a weeklong dislocation from home. Another 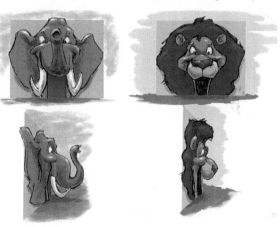 advantage, the facility will host two sets of campers every week.

We all agreed that animals would be a primary thematic element. Little kids love animals. The cabin groups will have animal names: lion, bear, elephant, etc., but, rather than a big sign on the cabin "LIONS" we all dreamed of huge, three-dimensional heads as the façade for each two-story cabin. I brought in my good friend Clark Tate to design the heads (see Clark's sketches, above) and everyone was *wild* about his work. We found a great company that fabricates dimensional creations for theme parks, etc. A sizable budget was set for the big animal façades, but the initial bid was bigger. Working with the fabricator, the camp director was able to adjust the scope of the big heads and the fabricator reduced their price. But it was still bigger than the budget. And … they still had a complete new camp to build—land to clear and prep, etc.

During our early brainstorming sessions I had told the director, Keith Oglesby, and his staff, the story of Pirates of the Caribbean growing well beyond its original scope. I encouraged Keith & Co. to dream big and we all did: There will be a water park in the center of camp, an eight-sided dining hall to be called the "Beastro," and a large gym/auditorium, but instead of being just a big box it will resemble Noah's Ark. There's a mini-golf, a giant play set ("The Jungle") and *more*! Still, the budget for the animal head façades was too small. Keith went back to his supportive and creative board. He was prepared to settle for painted façades, but, as I had told the staff at our first brainstorming session, "If the idea is good enough, sometimes the budget can get bigger (*more pirates*)."

Ten days ago Keith emailed to say that the board had increased their budget to fit the enormous dimensional heads for all twelve cabins. Remember this is a non-profit enterprise. Dream big then make your case passionately. We started brainstorming in 2009 and they greeted their first campers for the summer of 2012. You will find them on the web at *www.CarolinaCreek.org*. Look for my friend Clark's logo of their newest camp:

This is Your Brain as a Pirate

W!LD logo by ClarkTate.com

People who study functions of the brain tell us that on any given subject, an individual can have five hundred ideas.

That's one person opening the valve on their cerebral hard drive and executing a "cognitive dump" of all the stuff already filed away. If every member of a brainstorming team has *just* five hundred ideas on Canada Invasion, multiplied by seven team members, the creative process would begin with 3,500 ideas as kindling for the brainstorming bonfire you are building—just for starters. This is before we even begin to listen, react, and build on (*Yes, and …*) each other's ideas.

Brain watchers also point out that a brain, stimulated by sounds, music, fragrance, flavors (food and snacks), images, and other people's ideas, can expand as much as a thousand times per topic. Now your team has not a paltry 3,500 ideas, but 3,500 ideas times one thousand! Hmmm … 3,500 x 1,000 equals … carry the twenty-seven … let me see that's … *a whole lot of ideas*. (Three and a half million, actually!) Would three million *plus* be enough ideas to launch your company in Canada?

Mostly it's a matter of getting your analytical self (and inner critic) out of the way

(*No Blocking–No Wimping*) and allowing your natural creative spirit and curiosity to soar ... more, *more*.

I have used, to great effect, the technique of dividing a creative team into smaller groups of three to five and challenging them, "Who can come up with one hundred ideas quickest on the subject of _____." (Notice the goal is "one hundred" not "one hundred good, great, or *right*" ideas.) "You have five minutes ... GO!"

A good way to prevent team members from blocking their own ideas is to keep the pace brisk. Lots of ideas, quickly. Keep pushing to the last minute, whether you have one hour, a week, or just five minutes to imagine.

The next phases of Brainstorming/Creative Thinking have a voracious, insatiable appetite for ideas. So even when it seems as though you have *hatched* "enough," create *more*. If you push and push and push, you can get the most surprising *stuff* even in the last fifteen minutes of a four- or six-hour session by simply not thinking about it (not trying to figure out the "right" answer) and just blurting out everything that passes through your mind. Think, say, capture (write or sketch) until the last minute. Exhaustion is a helpful tool for getting at the wackiest ideas. Never be afraid of creating too many ideas. The more you create, the more raw material you will have to choose from during Critical Thinking, Agreement No. 7.

Doing Dream Work

Soon after leaving Imagineering and partnering to assist other enterprises, Max Miller and I were hired by former Disney cohort Jeffrey Katzenberg for a project at his then-new little outfit, Dreamworks SKG (formed with Steven Spielberg, Katzenberg, and record mogul David Geffen). Their electronic game division, Dreamworks Interactive, was developing a computer game as a companion to their animated feature *Prince of Egypt*, the biblical story of Moses (former shepherd). Jeffrey knew Max and I were creative and had a biblical bent.

At the end of a full day of Creative Thinking with the SKG team we had a pyramid full of ideas, but were stuck on making sense of the one concept we all liked most. It was quite complicated.

I took a stroll to the end of the hall to freshen up. In those short minutes a solution seemed to come my way. I was eager to try it out on this room full of playful thinkers.

Returning from the porcelain place I found the team disengaged, done for the day, and deciding on a dinner destination. Barely hinting at my new excitement, I took the sacred marker in hand and drew a quick picture of my idea for tracking Joseph's journey through a multidimensional, virtual environment. At the same time, it would track each player's unique experience. I believed it could be the key to unlock our complicated swirl of multi-dimensional time-travel occurring in layers of virtual environments. It took about a minute to lay out my plan. I set down the marker and stepped aside.

"You got that by going to the bathroom?" They liked it.

The VP asked Max, "Does he always do this?"

"Everyone does," said wise old Max.

Looking at me, the VP said, "Henceforth, we shall all go to the bathroom more!"

It wasn't the bathroom, or even me, especially. It was the end of the day when we had "stopped thinking." That is often a time when our minds are free to think about *anything.* In these moments of creative exhaustion we become free to no longer worry about figuring it out or getting the *right* answer. So I did a little "what if ..." exercise with myself.

There are always more ideas. I've participated in so many brainstorming sessions where the end-of-the-day-bathroom-visit produced only relief and clean hands. You never know when or where the next moment of inspiration may come. Take a walk. Splash some water on your face. Open a window. Open another window and stick your head out and take a deep breath. Repeat. Better yet, go outside. Have another cookie, tangerine, cup of Earl Grey—you know what works for you. (Scientifically, strawberries are the flavor that most stimulates creativity. Really. You can't make this stuff up. Well, I *can* ... but I didn't.)

Use all the time you have allotted for Creative Thinking. Keep pushing to the last minute. Then, just before adjourning, the facilitator says, "Five more ideas each. Go nuts."

After hundreds of failed attempts to perfect a working light bulb, Edison was successful. He wasn't finished, though: He spent the next forty years working to increase the average life of a bulb from forty hours to more than 1,500 hours. And he did it all in New Jersey!

Press on!

"It's kind of fun
to do the impossible."
Walt Disney

RECAP
 # Agreement No. 5: MORE IDEAS

- **Set outrageous goals** to keep things moving:
  - Fifty ideas on location. Where do we begin our invasion of Canada?
  - Fifty theme ideas. Military? Smugglers? International festival/street fair? Water carnival?
  - 10,000 spots to place your logo (guerrilla marketing)—"low-tack" adhesive. (Play with set time limits: five or seven minutes per exercise. Shorter is best.)
- **Work quickly.** The initial goal during Creative Thinking is **quantity: MORE!**
- **Take a breath, a bite, a walk,** refresh your mind, go outside. I used to surprise my teams at Imagineering with a mid-afternoon break. "Everyone into the van!" Our offices were just six blocks from the regional creamery for Baskin-Robbins, and they had a drive-up window!
- **Field Trip Ideas** to jump-start saggy imaginations and tired bodies.
- **Snacks.** Have mid-morning and mid-afternoon snacks brought in: sweet and savory; fruit, chips, cookies, power bars, juices ...
- **City Park.** Jump on a swing, a merry-go-'round, hide-n-seek, or play tug-o-war (especially with an invisible rope!).
- **Film** Watch a short, silly movie during snack (Buster Keaton, Marx Brothers, Laurel & Hardy, Mr. Bean, or the best of Lucy or Carol Burnett ...).
- **Story Time** Take turns bringing in (and reading aloud) an inspiring or amusing human interest story or children's book.
- **"Shakespeare Goes to H.R.":** Do a dramatic reading from your employee manual or the menu of a favorite eatery. Just a five-minute "Silly Break."
- **The Silly Game®:** "The silliest thing I can think of for this project is ..." Go around the room three times. At the end decide who had the silliest thought and give them five dollars from the blocking bowl.
- **The Last Five Minutes.** When you think you have thought of, said, and written down everything you can possibly imagine—and you are ready to give up—each team member gives three to five more ideas. You are beyond figuring it out. You no longer care about the quality of your ideas (or success). You just need to say five things ... **MORE.**

Shlubbing Along

We live in a world that has decided that a few, select, and special people have the corner on creativity and imagination while everyone else seems to be just shlubbing along.

Balderdash! Bilge, blather, and twaddle! I say.

That lie emanates from wherever God isn't. Every one of us is a glowing reflection of our Creator. Some glow brighter than others, at times. Some refuse to glow or, embarrassed by their own spark, hide it. Some feel that it isn't fair that one light may shine a bit brighter than others. That glow is evidence that we are all flares off the original spark—the Original Idea. A shimmer of the Eternal imagination goes on forever in each of us.

This goes triple for children, since they have not yet begun to self-censor, or believe the double-talk and drivel of doubt that we "grown-ups" have settled for. We adults have chosen to live every worry-plagued day of our lives guided more by what can't be—rather than inspired by what we can and might be. As someone has aptly observed, we do not live our dreams because we're too busy living our fears.

Children are born with a holy ignorance of Can't. They possess a blessed unfamiliarity with impossible. They traffic in Wonder and Try. Children constantly ask, "Why not?" The most useful item in their toolbox of learning is an unstoppable curiosity. As childlike curiosity wanes, learning begins to fade. Adults long ago stopped upending rocks just to say hello to the teeming kingdoms beneath. A bug's life no longer fascinates us. Sadly, nor does our own journey carry even a whiff of adventure anymore.

Real wisdom comes from what we learn after we "know everything." Pursuing "what's next?" and "what else is there?" fills the life of an "actively creative" person.

Now and then our child-like spirit sticks a foot in—or a nose out—and says, "I want to play too!" If we allow it—if we let down our grown-up guard—those original instincts we displayed as a child can and will re-emerge to sing, dance, cackle, shout, and explore the world. We were all told, too-young, to color inside the creativity crushing lines. The child you once were—and might yet be again—will not be careful, but sloppy and more than a bit reckless, because it genuinely doesn't matter. The sooner we stop worrying about so many things, the sooner we can more truly reflect our Maker and participate in making a difference. And not just in brainstorming sessions about our company's next big project.

For me, being in touch with my child-like Creator spirit is about taking the kind of risk that scares me—and often terrifies others. If my risks frighten you, that's as it should be. Your risks will frighten me. And so it goes.

I know when I'm in touch with my "inner child" because he keeps getting sent to my "inner principal." Still, that's a safe and familiar place for me, since in real life it was my father's office. From third through the eighth grades I attended a private school where my father was the principal. He was also one of my biggest cheerleaders—even when I got into the kind of trouble that got me sent to his office. Other kids were scared to be sent to "Mr. Wilson." But I knew my dad was like Aslan, the immense, roaring lion in C. S. Lewis's glistening and redemptive *Chronicles of Narnia*.

"Is he safe?" asked Lucy, inquiring about Aslan, the big lion.

"No," said Mr. Beaver. "But he's good."

Creativity won't always be safe. Risk takers need champions to stand up for them. We must all be champions for each other. Say, "Yes, and …" to the whim that's tiny as a phone doodle, as well as the notion as outrageous as setting a huge hotel down inside a theme park.

We champion one another to bring out the best of ourselves, collectively and individually. We cannot know when the next Emily Dickinson, Steve Jobs, or Walt Disney will come to invigorate our world with new thinking. So many possibilities might never have been realized if they had not walked among us.

We must not believe all the dreary dictums about what's appropriate, acceptable, reasonable, or even popular. All that hokum and hogwash about fitting in rather than sticking out comes from the dark side, the Prince of all Humbug. There are those who would like nothing *more* than for you and me to be *less*. The more we are all alike, all the same, the better it is for Old Scratch and his minions of mediocrity.

The more the Big Lie finds a home in our hearts and minds, the more we are diminished from making an essential contribution to the lives of others.

In the United States we celebrate and embrace people from hundreds of ethnic groups. Each makes its own glorious contribution to the unique fabric of our remarkable American culture. You need only look at the creativity in the colorful clothing of Mongolians, Kenyans, and Guatemalans; the amazing flavors from Tuscany, Thailand, and the Yucatan peninsula to see the rainbow contribution of the world's people groups to form a new color, the American culture. Sameness and carefulness infected none of these—and we are all the richer for their rule-breaking spirit of individuality. The addition of each of those ingredients makes our culture richer, fuller, and *more* tasty. More … everything!

Nonetheless, it doesn't take much to coax us into believing the lie that only a few among us *are* creative. If we accept that, then only a few us *will* be creative. Equality is no friend to creativity. We're getting flimflammed by the prince of all flummery. To be less creative is to be less human, less *you*.

An End to Flummery

This is the only life we have. I don't believe we get to come back and play with whoever Shirley MacLaine thinks she will be on her next visit. As far as I can tell, this is it, Virginia. There is no Santa, Elvis is dead, God is alive, and so are you—*if you choose to be*.

Don't think about whether you are creative or noncreative. Rather, ponder this for a moment: The human race is composed of several billion of us. People are actively and inactively creative throughout every waking moment of each day. We move back and forth on a continuum of creative activity and inspiration—at times effortlessly. "Hey, what's that over there?" Other times, creating can be very hard work. That's when we need more of each other most.

"I have no special talents. I am only passionately curious."

~ Albert Einstein

All that is asked is that you move from where you are toward where you might be. Even if you are an introvert, many await your vital participation—some need you to lead.

The symphony of human brilliance will be incomplete without your notes, played passionately.

If you feel inadequate, watch children. They are highly unskilled at pretty much everything they try. But they TRY EVERYTHING! They don't listen to maturity's hot air about being responsible, careful, or correct. Instead they fill their lives with hot dreams and imagination and fly to the stars. They don't get drunk on the moonshine of "act your age." They roll down grassy slopes, basking in the moon-glow and starlight of endless possibilities. Great dreamers have permanent grass stains on their pants from all that giggling and rolling down hills. Check the knees of your pants—right now. If there are no grass stains, go find the nearest high ground and start rolling. (If it is winter, a snow angel will do nicely.)

Stay curious.

Don't be afraid
to take a big step
if one is indicated.

You can't cross a chasm in two small jumps.

David Lloyd George
Prime Minister of Great Britain,
1916–1922

DONUTS ON THE MOON
[you wanna do what??]

When a new colleague of physicist Niels Bohr delivered an important speech to a group of their peers at the forefront of science, the speaker was curious as to how his presentation had been received by the other scientists.

Noticing Bohr and his colleagues huddled at the back of the room, the young scientist waited and then asked, "Do they think I'm crazy?"

"We all agree that your idea is crazy," Bohr said. "What divides us is whether it is crazy enough."

☞ Agreement No. 6: **WILD IDEAS**

"More" is never enough. As you are creating a mountain of ideas, be on the lookout for a particular kind of idea. It is neither good nor bad. It is WILD.

The 1947 leather-bound dictionary my father passed down to me records *wild* as "stormy, boisterous, unruly and marked by turmoil." That's a good start. WILD ideas are outrageous, impossible, untamed notions that probably make no sense at first—and will certainly cost *far too much*. (See "This Just In …" on *The W!LD* summer camp, pages 61-62.)

As often as not, WILD ideas feel embarrassing to speak aloud. And too often they aren't 'cause we BLOCK them from leaving our mind. But WILD ideas are the most likely to spark another team member, and another, and soon … we begin to recognize the value of saying whatever comes to mind—*everything*—however odd it may sound. Brainstorming affords the rarefied experience of speaking our first impressions and taking advantage of them. Go *Wild!*

Wild can be *expensive*, but often it is not. *Wild* may be something you don't know how to do—yet. Wild ideas live way out of bounds of everyday life. *Wild* makes people say, "We've never done it that way before!" How about this: *"If we really have never done this before, maybe now's the time!"* A wild idea may be something *"they* won't let you do" if you ask … so, don't ask.

When Michael Eisner asked us to brainstorm what we'd like to build in the old Disneyland parking lot I stepped to the big sheet where he'd drawn two big circles. (Top circle representing Disneyland park and the bottom circle one hundred acres of asphalt.) I drew a quick, pie-shaped wedge in the eleven o'clock position of the lower circle.

"Whatever we build. Let's put a hotel inside it," I said.

"Inside a theme park ... why?" asked a co-dreamer.

"Growing up in southern California, our family stayed at the Disneyland Hotel several times (across the street from the park). My brother and I would stand on the balcony and look across the street and try to imagine *what if* our hotel was right *inside* Adventureland or *on* Town Square, Main Street, USA? How cool would that be?"

They got it. (They were Imagineers.)

Trust me. The idea of placing a big resort hotel *inside* a theme park was not only unpopular at first, especially with hotel builders and management—from inside Disney. But the idea was too good to die. Eventually, because it fit so well into the final concept for a California-themed park, they couldn't *not* build the Grand Californian Hotel inside that park.

When Disney's California Adventure theme park opened in February 2001, there it was, the Grand Californian Hotel ... inside the park. Step out the back door of the hotel and you are inside a theme park. That wild idea worked: in fall 2009 Disney added two hundred rooms and fifty vacation villas (timeshare) for Disney Vacation Club members.

Wild Ideas can be the boot that kicks open an old, locked door to a place we've never been—or haven't visited in a long time. We usually start with ideas we think make the most sense. Fine. Get them out of your head. But if we keep pushing, we'll move past "sense" to "surprise." Don't be afraid or embarrassed to offer the most unlikely or ridiculous whim. That's the nature of wild ideas.

The alternative to wild is "good" ideas. These are the safe, instantly-accepted-by-all ideas that fail to stimulate, inspire, or innovate. "Good ideas" almost never overcome your competition. Because the "other guys" are going to do *wild*. Bet on it.

Steve Jobs had a simple, wild idea when he broke the mold of computers being gray, beige, or "putty." Apple introduced the teal "Bondi Blue" iMac in 1998. In no time, office supply barns were filled with every known office device from wastebaskets to staplers in blue and eventually a rainbow of colors to match Apple's phalanx of festive iMacs. Up to that point the world had lived with black and gray office accessories. And the iMac begat the iPod, iPhone, iPad—and in 2011 little upstart Apple's profitability surpassed the behemoth of Redmond. Microsoft is now Microsecond. Apple has twice surpassed Exxon as America's biggest public company. That's WILD.

Pirates of the Caribbean (the ride) filled its first boatload of Disneyland guests in 1967. Nearly fifty years later it remains one of the longest lines in four Magic Kingdoms, on three continents, nearly every day. The daily "To-Do" list of your average pirate was hardly the stuff of family vacations—until 1967. And the worldwide gross for the four *Pirates* movies is $3.7 billion (as of January, 2012).

WILD ideas are precisely the sort of ideas that will serve best to create your Canada

Invasion. (Pirates ... riding dinosaurs.) Wild ideas are the most likely to stimulate the energy and imagination of other team members (as well as numerous business partners and vendors). This WILD-ness can generate enthusiasm that will carry through the life of the project and transfer to the public image of your product or service.

Wild ideas express an optimism that believes in the imagination and brilliance of the others—including

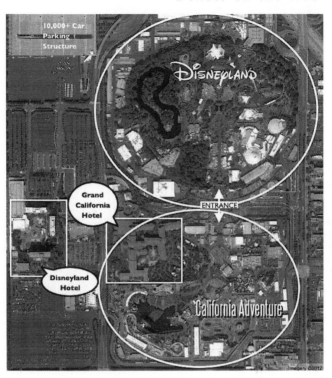

your customers. (Don't miss the last chapter of this book.) A wild idea announces, "I came to play. Jump in!" And if it is WILD enough, they will say, "YES, and ... I'll take three!"

Creative Thinking is merely *words*, sketches, cartoons, doodles, and thought fragments. They are IDEAS born in the imagination. They really do not *yet* exist. As ideas, they are harmless—and FREE. Even when my architect friends build models, those are not yet the real place. They are sketching in 3-D.

It costs nothing to take a flight of the imagination over the largest cities in Canada and imagine a group of fifty parachutists with your logo descending upon those vast populations. That exercise might lead you to a major aerial assault with antique biplanes, bombers, and blimps filling the midday skies over Montreal, Toronto, Vancouver, and Winnipeg ...

Whether it's a major product launch (invading a country) or dreaming in the middle of the dirt lot or empty building where your new company headquarters (or plant, clinic, retail center, restaurant, college, church, or community center) will be housed, WILD will inspire thinking that can forge revolutionary results that your old, safe "kicking around a few ideas" system never could have imagined.

Go *WILD* ... and stay there for a bit.

What's Wild?

Most folks are too careful—self-editing any wild, silly, impossible ideas that spark in their mind. We decide it's a no-go, and we never share it out loud. The key is to use *everything* and *anything*.

We rarely let WILD ideas escape the prison of our cautious, too-timid minds. I encourage groups at the end of a long brainstorming day to give the "Wildest Idea of the Day Award." (Go ahead and award the Blocking Bowl bucks; you will easily refill the bowl again tomorrow.)

> "Humanity has advanced, when it has advanced, not because it has been sober, responsible, and cautious, but because it has been playful, rebellious, and immature!"
>
> Tom Peters, author/business leader
> *In Search of Excellence* and *Re-Imagine!*

Doing this work with a wide array of clients across the corporate landscape—in Europe and the Americas—I have learned valuable lessons. I have gained insights about the creative process, as a team effort, from every conceivable profession, including:

- bankers
- marketing and PR firms
- educators (all levels)
- medical professionals
- writers
- ministers
- camping professionals
- law enforcement
- restauranteurs
- performing arts organizations
- seminarians
- parents
- movie and television studios
- commercial and industrial real estate developers
- electrical engineers
- folks in space and defense programs
- entertainment conglomerates
- designers
- musicians
- printers
- publishers and editors
- university faculties
- elementary school children
- theatre artists
- and even attorneys

All were challenged to tackle life with re-ignited imaginations, purposeful passion, and unceasing curiosity. Many have done so eagerly—*wildly*. But too many have been reluctant, even resistant, to try.

Attorneys, McNair? How do you do creativity with lawyers?!

Even for a Creative Thinking session, the corporate world has difficulty disengaging their brains from the practical, the nuts-n-bolts concerns of their daily work life. They become bogged down by the boundaries of sensible thinking, practicality, calendars, and budgets.

"Will it work?" and "Can we afford it?" are the default settings for the corporate mind.

Do not let the money, the schedule, and a litany of questions about feasibility hobble the creative efforts of any team. Money is not only the root of all evil, it is a demonic force in the creative process.

How do we even **do that?**

What will it cost?

That will take forever.

No WILD ideas, please.

But we have to be WILD. Non-*Wild* has already been done to death—both by us and our competitors. It takes *Wild* just to get traction today. Wild shakes up the marketplace, wakes up consumers, and crushes competition. Go Wild—Go Now!

Brainstorming is a lot like t-ball and Las Vegas: "**Everybody plays!**"

⑨ TRY THIS

Distribute HATCH! (introducing the **7 Agreements of Brainstorming** to your entire staff). Put it forward as the working language for day-to-day interaction in emails, text messages, voice mail, meetings, hallway encounters, and break–time banter. At some point in the coming months consider including **every employee** in a brainstorming session. Even an hour of brainstorming on "How might we improve the working environment around here?" will go a long way to improving teamwork, and creating more positive, proactive communications. It **will** boost morale while teaching a new way of problem solving, out loud. It will do nothing less than create a new way of communicating for your entire staff, all the time. Folks will learn to use these agreements every day, over lunch and under pressure. It only takes a few, using the agreements, to lead the way for all others.

One of the first calls I received, post-Imagineering, was from a company that had fifty-one donut shop/bakeries in a three-state region. The CEO asked to have lunch together.

"I need to turn you loose on my management team," he said. "They are stuck on *good* and need shaking up to get to the next level."

"Great," I said.

"Yup. We need to get to great."

"Or beyond?" I said.

He had a strong executive team, but they were numbed by the daily pursuit of

practicality and efficiency. *Wild* was not in their orbit.

Their struggle with WILD thinking drove me to invent, on the spot, a new teaching tool. It would transport practical minds across time to a new and as-yet-unimagined future. They needed to disengage from the constricted criteria óf *how to get there* and imagine a much better, more exciting and creative organization. Tired, old strategic planning would not get them to where their rule-breaking CEO wanted to go. He had an actively creative mind but did not want to be dictator. He believed in their brilliance.

We parceled the group of about thirty into smaller teams of four or five, with a cross-section of field managers and top execs in each group—carefully separating the *three* eggs: CEO, President, and CFO into different groups.

First, I offered simple instructions for this new exercise I had HATCHed in my head moments before.

Newsletter of the Future®

"Write the headlines for your company's *Newsletter of the Future*®. Create a list of *fifty* headlines for your company newsletter in the year (current year + twenty). Imagine only the BIG STORY, not *how* it happened. Don't worry about how you're going to get there from here. You are just saying, "It is now the year 20___ (now + 20) and *this* is what we're doing. Just headlines. Snappy, brief, wild. Got it? Go!"

What followed was an outbreak of *serious crazy.* The room filled with loud and the people turned silly, animated, and excited—well beyond anything they had shown all morning. Virtually everyone jumped into the fray! This is the nonlinear, playful chaos of WILD, creative thinking. I found myself giggling just watching them. The ideas were flowing so rapidly, that a couple of groups had two people writing simultaneously! I had planned their journey to the future to last twenty minutes; I blew the whistle after less than ten. They had broken out of the self-imposed bonds of careful, rational thinking.

Newsletter of the Future® freed them from the prison of the practical: *how* and *how much.* They didn't give a flying bran muffin about *how*—for now.

As each team read aloud a few ideas from their list, their mood was radiant—a stark contrast to the sobriety that had marked much of the morning. After I had filled one big sheet with a sampling of twenty-five to thirty of their headlines I asked, "Look at this list. What percentage of these are possible right now, *this year*—not five, ten, or twenty years into the future? What can we do *now?*"

"We could do 10 percent now." (From the ever-cautious chief financial officer.)

"Fifty percent." From a district manager.

"All of 'em!" The commissary manager shouted. He was at the helm of the daily baking of every item sold in all fifty-one locations in three states.

"Great!" I said. "Look at the list. Are there any ideas that are impossible right now?"

All eyes searched the list we had created from their various team lists. Was there a deal-breaker? An idea that was *too* wild? They were up for anything and weren't waiting twenty years to break through to great.

Then, there it was, mid-list, a certifiably undoable concept. I read it out loud ... and circled it.

Donuts on the moon.

A mixture of laughter and looks of *Okay, McNair. Now what?* Do we cross it off the list?

"Donuts on the moon!" I proclaimed. "We've *already* been to the moon. We send folks into space all the time. Heck, they *live* there now, and they don't eat meatloaf in a tube anymore."

Directly in front of me sat the head croissant: their CEO.

"Louis," I asked my friend, "what would you be willing to pay NASA to have your baked goods on the next space shuttle?"

He answered so quickly you might have suspected we had rehearsed our interchange. "They couldn't name a price that would be too high!"

"One million dollars," I said.

"Done," he said, defiantly.

"What!?" The purse-guarding CFO joined in.

"Anthonyyyyyy?!!" The CEO shot back at his younger, fiscally stringent brother. *"Donuts on the moon!"*

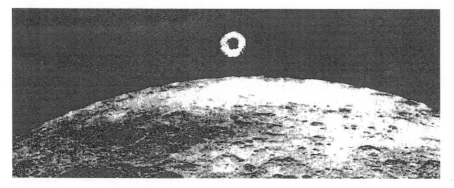

"*Two* million!" Anthony raised the stakes.
Big, doughy laughter all around.
"Gentlemen, start your ovens!" I shouted. "We're going *to the moon!*"

Try this: Write your own, personal "Newsletter of the Future." (Just the headlines.) Can you recall any life goals or personal dreams from ten or twenty years ago? How'd you do? What will you be up to in the year 20__? Think wild.

> ⑨ **DreamComeTrue**   Life has lots of twists and turns, job changes, new residences, finding a new dry cleaner. We don't always have a say in the changes in our life. It's good to have a few dreams tucked in our back pocket—or on TODAY's To-Do list—that we have control over. I had dreamed of working at Disney Imagineering since I was twelve. Once there, I didn't stay as long as I'd hoped to, but every day I was there was a dream come true. Imagineering prepared me for the work I do now with a stunning variety of clients. My life these days is filled with work I could NEVER have dreamed of doing.

Now Leaving the Magic Kingdom

Because of my experience in live theater, one of the questions posed to me by Imagineers on my first day at Imagineering (when my SAK Theatre partner Herb Hansen and I were consultants) was, "Would it be possible to use live actors as an integral part of major attractions?"

They really did not know the answer. Imagine Pirates of the Caribbean with a few key robots replaced by *live* actors and you get a glimpse of the changed focus of theme park design when we began working on the Disney–MGM Studios in Florida (now called Disney's Hollywood Studios).

We opened Disney-MGM Studios, Orlando, in May 1989 with live performers as

integral show elements in every major brick-and-mortar attraction. More than twenty years later, those elements are all still in place. I participated in the brainstorming of this entire project (theme park and working studio) from the beginning—when it was literally a blank piece of paper. Very quickly, my focus became to head up the development of all *live* elements in the park's major attractions. It was a heady time. My "Streetmosphere" program—a.k.a. "Citizens of Hollywood"—became a surprise hit along with the enormously popular Adventurers Club and the Comedy Warehouse at Pleasure Island—Disney's first evening entertainment district.

Thus, I was promoted to Director, creating the Live Show Development department inside Imagineering. My new "live show design" group would be an Imagineering resource for all project teams. (We did not do lip-syncing, clean-cut, college kids tap-dancing in front of castles. We did *actors* in attractions.)

Not much more than a year after my promotion, I was stunned when my mentor, Disney Imagineering chief Marty Sklar, decided to buy me out of my contract. He said it was time to push me out of the large and very comfortable Disney nest. I was receiving more and more speaking invitations for my creativity presentations to corporate gatherings outside Disney. Marty knew that untethered independence would free me of conflicts of interest and allow me to expand my speaking and consulting endeavors.

I can't say I was happy about leaving. I was a *Disney Imagineer*—a lot of my identity had been wrapped up in my years at the dream factory. But Marty was convinced it was time for me to move on. He wasn't wrong. It has always been important for me to do work that *challenges* the best parts of me and allows me to make a *contribution* to projects larger than myself. Those were my goals when I arrived at Disney in 1982; those are my goals today. It was a sweet and celebratory parting that I'll always remember (Okay, it was bittersweet. I've learned to appreciate that distinction in chocolates and fond farewells).

My first Monday away from Imagineering, I received unsolicited calls from four other theme park design groups, including Disney rival Universal Studios. I told all who called that I was very interested, but I was taking a month off to do *nothin'!* (This was the brilliant advice of Tim Swift, my longtime good friend and really smart guy.)

A month later, all four companies called back, plus a few others. Among them was my old Imagineering chum Jeff Kurti, now at Disney Studios. It seemed that Disney CEO Michael Eisner had his own authentically *WILD idea*. Michael thought that the two dozen Disney divisions ought to talk to each other and even—wait for it—*work* together. Such a knucklehead, Michael Eisner—always on a quest for the next impossible dream. He achieved a lot of them.

The plan was to convene a series of interdepartmental idea-sharing sessions as a regularly occurring conversation woven into Disney's corporate fabric. Michael Eisner's newly forged Office of Corporate Synergy would be the catalyst for these gatherings. To launch this strategy, the studio hired me to facilitate six weeks of brainstorming sessions that involved middle and upper management from every outpost of the Kingdom that Walt built (and Michael renovated). Our first project, a PR time bomb: the "Mouses," Mickey and Minnie, were about to turn sixty-five years old. How do we put a positive Disney spin on "old mice"?

Playful, Rebellious, and Immature

I kicked off the first "Mickey & Minnie at 65" Creative Thinking sessions by reading from an internal memo: "Mickey has just been signed as *spokes–mouse* for *Depends*, adult diapers."

(Pause for effect.)

"Any other ideas?" I said.

Not everyone found the memo hilarious. Fortunately, "The Boss" liked it. Michael liked that one a lot. In fact, after the first session Michael insisted I open every session that first week with the "diaper deal." He laughed at each new group's reactions and roared at their non-reactions and scowls.

"I'll take Rebellious for 200, Alex."

"That's not funny," one division poo-bah said.

"No, Ed, it's hilarious," said another.

The Depends memo (a fake) was way too wild for some, but it kicked open the "Don't Go There" door and raised the "Anything Goes" banner over the S.S. Synergy.

That really Wild (and not just a little silly) idea turned out to be a great brainstorming ice breaker—which took on an air of urgency when everyone realized Mickey and Minnie really were not getting any younger.

"Now what are we gonna do about that?"

McNair at 40

Speaking of getting older … let's. Here are two of my favorite Wild thinking moments—two of my birthdays.

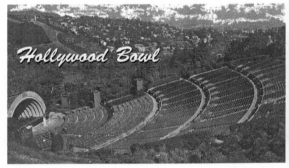

A birthday party on a BIG stage :: On Saturday afternoon, January second, two days before my thirtieth birthday, a small contingent of longtime friends picked me up to go to lunch at my favorite old Hollywood eatery, Musso & Franks. (President Polk ate there. Really.) This old-world restaurant is home to the surliest waiters west of the Hudson River. On our way, we stopped by the Hollywood Bowl to "pick up a friend who was there rehearsing."

It was all a setup, a ruse, a sting, a lie. The Hollywood Bowl is a 16,000-seat amphitheater owned by the city of Los Angeles. We were met there by nearly three dozen of my best longtime friends and family who came from Washington State, San Diego, and all points in between—everyone wearing a distinctive hat.

We took a photo of all of us standing on the Hollywood Bowl stage, surrounding the **"Please Keep Off the Stage"** sign. (See photo on next page.) A wonderful celebration in every way.

A Birthday of Olympic Proportions

Ten years hence, determined to have another one-of-a-kind birthday bash, I thought long and hard: What place best represents forty? Forty miles at sea, 40,000 feet in the air, the

Hollywood Bowl birthday gang. That's me, standing center with beard. My mom and dad (top hat) are at my immediate right.

fortieth parallel, and then ... a *forty-yard line*—the Rose Bowl, just 4.2 miles from my home in Pasadena. A quick call would seal the deal.

"Rose Bowl, good afternoon."

"Is the Rose Bowl available on Saturday, January fourth?"

"January coming up?"

"Right. How much to rent it?"

"It's $6,000 a day or $4,000 for half a day."

"Is that the new math they teach in the Pasadena schools?"

"That's the price, sir."

I told her about the Hollywood Bowl, hoping to enroll her in my dream of cake and friends on the forty-yard line. She wasn't biting.

I was tempted to hang up and walk across Mar Vista Avenue and two houses down to my friend and neighbor Rick Cole—*da Mayor* of Pasadena—and ask for a favor. Concluding my dead-end chat with Little Miss No's Bowl, I made a mental note: *Never start by asking "how much."* After all, there are other forty-yard lines in LA.

I'd try one more option before visiting Mayor Rick across the street.

A second call. (Ringing, ringing.)

"Good morning, Los Angeles Memorial Coliseum."

"Hello. Is the Coliseum available on Saturday, January the fourth?"

"Let me check ... ah ... nothing booked."

"I need a forty-yard line."

"*Which one?*"

"Is one of them already booked?"

"*What's this for?*"

I recounted the Hollywood Bowl bash, ten years earlier, as I had for the Rose Queen, hoping for a better outcome. "I'd like to serve birthday cake to a few friends on the forty-yard line for my fortieth."

(Silence. Then ...)

"*That's #@&% great!* (Laughing heartily.) *We gotta do this! Who are you?!*"

"Craig McNair Wilson."

"*Got it. How long do you want the place?*"

(He said "place" like I was renting the back room at IHOP for a Boy Scout breakfast.)

"How about noon to four."

"*Great. We're closed that day, so ... I'll have to pay a custodian to unlock a gate—$35 an hour, four-hour minimum.*"

"I'll take the full minimum."

"*Got it!*"

"$140 and ... ?" (I'm thinking, *Down from $6,000 at the Pasadena Rose the price too high Bowl!*)

"Is there anything else?" I said.

"*Maybe a small user's fee?*"

"Okay." (I hoped he would say only a thousand dollars. Remember, I still hadn't asked the actual cost of renting the *Los Angeles Memorial Coliseum*.) "How much user's fee?"

"*Is a hundred bucks all right?*"

"That'll be just fine." (My mind was dancing. I wanted to spike my checkbook in the end zone!)

"*Okay. Noon to four, Saturday, January fourth. Birthday ... Wilson, party of ... How many are you expecting?*"

"What's the place hold?"

"*Total numbered seats is 92,753. How many are you inviting?*"

"If everyone shows up we'll have 92,600 *empty* seats. May I come down and look the place over?"

"*Haven't you ever been here?*"

Of course I had. Next day, I was sitting in a golf cart, field level, in the Los Angeles Memorial Coliseum.

"I was here in 1959 for closing day of the Billy Graham crusade—largest crowd ever here, I think."

"*Yup. There's a giant, bronze plaque on the wall, up there in the archway.*"

"So ... will my party be the smallest official event—"

"*You make the plaque, I'll put it up myself, Mr. Wilson.*"

On Saturday, January 4, 1992, a custodian with 127 keys and forty-some new friends from across the years enjoyed birthday cake on the forty-yard line of the *Los Angeles Memorial Coliseum*. There was touch football, Frisbees, and music. My ubiquitous friend

Maxwell J. Miller captured the entire event on video with one-on-one interviews of everyone telling "*How I met McNair.*"

The two phone calls to secure a place for the event—my fortieth birthday party—illustrate the heart of the **7 Agreements of Brainstorming** process. The queen of the Rose Bowl **BLOCKED** my creative thinking and punctured my dream—momentarily. Then the light changed. The guy at the Coliseum "got it" and we **YES, AND**-ed our way to a **WILD** deal. Both conversations occurred within the same hour.

Sitting on the team bench of the Coliseum, my lifelong friend Josh asked, "What does it cost to rent this place, McNair?"

I deferred the question to my pal Tim, who stages large entertainment and marketing events worldwide: "Take a guess, Mr. Swift."

"Hmmm" Tim surveyed the vast stadium. "It probably starts at fifteen [thousand], and McNair worked his magic, so, I'll guess you got it for five."

"I never asked the price till we had a deal," I said. "The base fee to rent the *Los Angeles Memorial Coliseum* starts at *twenty thousand dollars* per day—unfurnished." I told them about the Rose Bowl bungle and then said, "I rented this joint for two-hundred-forty bucks."

"*Two-hundred-forty bucks?!!!*" They roared. "A miracle ... impossible."

And so it came to pass that my fortieth birthday was convened on the forty-yard line of the **only** stadium in the *world* that has hosted *two* modern Olympic Games—1932 and 1984—and *my* birthday!

All *three* events were a rousing success. Billy Graham did pretty good there as well.

Donuts on the moon, a birthday in the L. A. Coliseum, a bigger hole in the ground filled with MORE pirates, or a summer camp for six year olds with two-story animal heads and a giant Noah's ARKenasium. What WILD ideas are *you* holding back? What are you *thinking* that you

"McNair at 40" Los Angeles Memorial Coliseum :: Many of the same friends who were at the Hollywood Bowl surprise thirtieth birthday bash came for cake on the forty-yard line—ten years later—at the L. A. Coliseum. Most of the teenagers above were the little kids at the Bowl. (Notice the giant "40" on grass in front of group.)

should be *saying* to your team *out loud?* What is *donuts on the moon* for your organization? Apply *that* to your Canada Invasion.

Anything goes. Most folks are too careful. We self-edit any wild, silly, impossible ideas that come to mind. (That's you BLOCKING *you.*) We'll bite our tongue before uttering a really wild idea out loud, risking embarrassment. Let WILD escape the prison of your overly cautious mind. Aim for terrifying, untamed, ridiculous, and outrageously expensive. You've done **possible**—even difficult—a lot. Time to try **impossible.** When time comes to invade Canada, everyone will ask, "How did you **ever** come up with this idea? It's so ... weird, wacky, **wild,** and wonderful."

GO WILD! Leave now.

RECAP
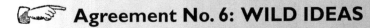 # Agreement No. 6: WILD IDEAS

Anything goes. Whatever comes to your mind, SAY IT. (Don't you BLOCK you.)

- **WILD ideas are a vital ingredient** to successful brainstorming (and vital to successful marketing, sales, new product development, corporate identity redesign, dynamic office décor, inspiring leadership ...)
- **WILD ideas are expensive, impossible, and embarrassing** to say out loud—at first.
- **"How?" and "How Much?" can not be a part** of the Creative Thinking process. (If someone offers an idea and no one can imagine how it could be done, head that way!)
- **If you could do ANYTHING** (on this project) what would **you** do?
- **If FAILURE were not possible**, what would you do?
- **If you had unlimited RESOURCES** (including budget), then what?
- **Newsletter of the Future®**—imagine twenty years hence, what will your organization be doing? Do it NOW! (I'll bring the donuts.)

THE ART OF BEING WISE IS THE ART OF KNOWING WHAT TO OVERLOOK.

William James
Psychologist, author
(1842-1910)

IT'S A MENU, NOT A BALLOT

Time to decide. We have reached the final step in the brainstorming process (cue drum roll): CRITICAL THINKING! This is where the cream rises to the top. We re-focus our thinking and select the ideas that will take us where we want to go. During Critical Thinking, we'll abandon hundreds, even thousands of ideas we imagined during Creative Thinking—and expand the ideas that deliver the goods. As we plan and implement our Canada Invasion, this is the last step of brainstorming. (Planning and implementation will come next. As the saying goes, "The reward for hard work is more work.")

(You will find practical tools for planning and implementation in the second part of this book—after the intermission.)

Now, though, Brainstorming's *final* agreement:

☞ Agreement No. 7: **CRITICAL THINKING**

As a theatrical director, I give verbal *notes* to cast, crew, and design teams at the beginning and end of each day's rehearsal. These contain observations for adjustments to improve performances, as well as technical, and design elements. My comments are *critical,* which means they are a product of my analysis toward accomplishing a better result. I make an evaluation as to quality and effectiveness.

Giving notes must not mean that I am judgmental in a mean-spirited or arrogant way. To have value, my critiques must be constructive, informative, understandable, and above all doable. Otherwise they are just a scold. My observations must "serve the work" and make our production stronger, richer, smarter, more engaging. A director's notes are worthless, hollow words if they don't move us all toward greater artistic achievement. This would be true for anyone in a supervisory position in any organization.

That's Critical Thinking. It's not about trashing worthless ideas. Instead it's about selecting ideas worthy of expanding upon because they contribute to the end result we're imagining together.

In brainstorming we talk about Critical Thinking as focused analytical evaluation, and purposeful thinking with a concise *direction,* a clear *objective* to serve the project.

Direction: Canada.

Objective: At this point our target topic begins to take shape, and it soon begins to resemble the final outcome. Critical Thinking will lead to the project's Planning and Implementation phases.

Making a Smaller Target

By now, your team has endless lists and walls filled with doodles and ideas to choose from. How do we begin narrowing our choices? In too many brainstorming sessions I have seen

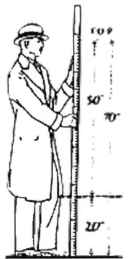

facilitators go to the wall of words-n-doodles and ask (pointing to one idea), "Who likes this idea? Hands." Counting raised hands, the facilitator writes the number next to that idea. Then she asks, "Who does *not* like this idea?" and writes the number of "yays and nays." And so on to the next idea, and the next—on every list. This can take days (and feel like decades).

That is a pointless exercise, accomplishing nothing. Why isn't this an effective way to weed through all the ideas—to decide which are good and which to set aside?

It would seem so, but it's not. Decades of doing this has taught me that it's useless—a tedious and painful waste of time. It can even be destructive. Each idea was the suggestion of an individual. And though you may not recall who said it, rest assured that most team members will remember many of the ideas they contributed. This "voting" process converts Blocking to a group project. At it's worst, it becomes full-contact spiritual abuse. Making it a faux-democratic exercise does *not* make it less abusive. Instead of one person not liking an idea, there are now five people who think it's a crack-brained dud. It's emotional piling-on. Stop it!

Critical Thinking Is Not a Ballot, It's a Menu

It does not matter which ideas we DO NOT like. What matters is selecting ideas that work best for the objectives of this project. Ignore the ones that don't; they're not necessarily bad ideas, they're just not the right ideas now. Like my notes to actors and designers, Critical Thinking must focus on what sparks further creativity, enthusiasm, and forward movement for *this* project.

There is a faster, more positive, playful, and productive way to approach Critical Thinking. Since you posted all your lists around the room as you went along, every idea should be visible to all. During *Critical Thinking* every idea may now be considered—and expanded upon. We won't use everything we have imagined in the final plan for our Invasion, but everything is available. We are putting together a puzzle. Our thousands of ideas, thoughts, off-handed remarks, doodles, and stuff we ripped out of a magazine and pinned to the wall are all potential ingredients—from small notions to the wild, weird, and wacky.

First, remember *Agreement No. 2: Separate Two Eggs.* (If you haven't recently done so, take a break.)

🔥 **Try this:** Facilitator says, "Let's take a break. When we get back, we'll begin Critical Thinking. Take a quick scan through our lists of ideas during the break to refresh your memory. When we reconvene, we'll begin narrowing the list and focus our brainstorming on some of our favorite concepts. So get something to drink, grab a snack, and look around the room for long lost gems and buried treasure."

Critical Thinking (3 steps)

1. GRAB

Facilitator: "Call out an idea you would like to expand upon for our Canada Invasion. This is not a trick question. It's not what you like *best*, *most*, or *if you could only pick one*—we're just looking for one idea to start pulling together. Grab one you like."

"I like that giant, downtown, street party idea," Herb says. (Life's always a party for Herb.)

"I'm drawn to the one hundred parachuters—*in five cities*—event," says MJ. (He likes a spectacle.)

"Sir! I still want the mock military invasion thing, Sir!" That from the ever-silly Sara (no "H").

The facilitator selects one of these to begin Critical Thinking.

Street Party.

GRAB a more specific, narrowly focused version of your target to launch your company in Canada. So now you narrow the creative conversation from *Canada Invasion* product launch to "Canada *Street Party* Launch." When you GRAB this idea, you are not deciding this is it, you are merely selecting one theme or idea to brainstorm in a more focused way. You are still creating an event for launching your company's products or services into the Canadian market, but for the next little while you will be designing a street party to accomplish that launch.

At the top of a new sheet, write **Canada Street Party Launch** in big, bold letters.

2. GROUP

Facilitator: "Scan all the ideas on all our lists and locate *any* and *all* ideas that fit into a *Street Party* theme." Start by rediscovering the ideas that came as a result of people using "Yes, and …" when the *street party* idea was first suggested. Take all ideas that connect with *street party* and **GROUP** them all on the new list.

Many ideas are generic, like *international theme*, which could fit into *street party*, *parachute drop*, *music festival*, or just about any other concept for your launch. Grouping similar ideas begins to create a larger and more specific picture of the project's ultimate shape as a Street Party.

3. GROW

Facilitator: "Now we're going to use **The 7 Agreements of Brainstorming** to imagine our Canada launch specifically as a street party. We have grouped dozens of ideas we hatched already. Now we will be creating and expanding upon them by **GROW**ing the event with our new, more-focused theme. All Agreements still apply: *"Yes, and ..."*, *No Blocking/No Wimping*, *More ideas* (more than just the ones Grabbed and Grouped from existing lists), and *Wild ideas*—wilder than anything on the walls ... so far.

Brainstorming the Canada launch as a street party may create renewed energy and could go on for a while. The facilitator must gauge the creative enthusiasm of the team and decide how long to press on this topic. As long as ideas are flowing, keep after it—keep Growing.

When the team starts running out of street party ideas, the facilitator will say, "Three more ideas from each person, quickly."

Next, GRAB another idea from all your existing lists—*aerial invasion* (MJ's parachute assault on major cities in Canada). GROUP all ideas relating to this topic from your lists and GROW (brainstorm) that group of ideas on a new sheet with the heading "Canada Launch Aerial Invasion." Include any ideas from the *street party* group that would also work for aerial invasion. Add them to the new list. Someone may suggest the aerial invasion could be the finale to the idea of a faux military parade. Brainstorm the idea of combining two or more concepts.

Repeat the three steps of Critical Thinking—GRAB, GROUP, and GROW—on as many ideas as time and team energy allow.

You won't have to force it. Great ideas will prove themselves robust and dynamic by the number of supporting ideas they attract.

In Critical Thinking—as with Creative Thinking—*inertia* and enthusiasm are key. So keep the process moving forward. **Even if the first Group of ideas or theme is great— overwhelmingly and enthusiastically embraced by the team—DON'T STOP. Grab, Group, and Grow at least three themes.**

If you generate as many as five themes, consider breaking into small groups (even adding a few staff members who have not yet been involved). Quickly catch them up on the Canada launch and tell them, "We are creating a giant street party." If the original team had seven people, be sure to include one or two of those folks in each new team of five to seven for continuity and explain work done so far. Give each team one theme to further expand on. "As many ideas as you can imagine in thirty minutes."

If your first Critical Thinking session produces a concept that all agree is **great**, pat yourself on the back, then go for another round. Set the first topic aside and move to a second theme. The first theme will survive the competition and development of other topics that you Grow.

As a facilitator, I often start the brainstorming of each new "Group" with "Okay, that was great, but the NEXT ONE will be it. **This one** will be the one!" (Even if we do five rounds, five topics.) This serves as a challenge and builds enthusiasm for each new topic. I will even challenge teams to make the next topic greater, more fun, WILDer. How can we make Idea No. 5: *Canada Water Festival Launch* the WILDest concept?

As you begin to GRAB topics for more specific brainstorming you may identify multiple topics the team wants to GROUP and GROW. To maximize your time, break into teams of three to five, with each team brainstorming a *different* topic. When the street party team comes back with lots of new ideas, others can still contribute even more ideas to GROW the concept.

As you GRAB each new topic from your brainstorming lists, you are in essence starting the brainstorming process over. But this time you have thousands of ideas already available around the room. All of these are resources for the task ahead. You can GROUP as many of those as might work with each newly focused target topic. As with Creative Thinking, you do not have to be correct during Critical Thinking. You are still brainstorming—but with more focus on specific theme.

It's up to the facilitator to keep pushing the team on each topic as long as the process stays fruitful. Then it's time to say, "Okay, that's one set of ideas—one theme—now let's move on to another concept for our Canada launch. Someone GRAB another topic."

When your team isn't sparking to the current topic, leave it and "GRAB, GROUP, and GROW" a different one.

What if somebody Grabs a stupid topic to Grow during critical thinking? Simple: Grow for it! See where it leads …

My experience shows that weak, "dumb," thin, and "stupid" ideas ("Corduroy Invasion") will fade, fizzle, or die from lack of enthusiasm, or interest. This can even happen with an idea that, when it was suggested, seemed *great*. And great things can also come from an idea that may, at first, seem simple if even foolish. Grab it and play with it awhile—five minutes or ten quick ideas on the topic from each team member. See if you can Grow it into something workable, interesting, or fun. Treat it like a game. If you cannot, then pick a different idea to GROW. Team-building will occur even when working on something mundane—if everyone is contributing with the same level of attack.

Critical Thinking can even take the impossible or ridiculous and transform it to a workable concept, even something great.

This Stupid Elevator is Brooooooooken!

When Michael Eisner was wooing Mel Brooks to move his production company, Brooksfilms, to the Disney Studios lot in Burbank, he brought Mel over to Imagineering. Mel and his son, Max, love Disneyland. I was charged with assembling a small team of my fellow concept designers to meet with Mel, Michael, and Marty (Sklar), chief of Imagineering.

"Lets do a Mel Brooks attraction for Disney–MGM Studios, Florida," Michael said.

"How do we do that?" Mel asked immediately.

"McNair?" my boss, Marty, prodded.

"Well, Mr. Brooks ..."

"Call me, Mel," he said. "And you are ...?" (Looking at my name tag.)

"I'm Mr. *Wilson.*" He laughed big and we were off to grand start. (I recall he also slapped me, playfully.)

"Think of it as telling a great Mel Brooks story," I said. "But instead of telling it in moving images projected on a wall, we tell it with concrete walls and the technology of modern theme parks: Audio-animatronics, high-tech ride vehicles, Pepper's Ghost ..."

"Who's Pepper?" Mel asked.

"Doesn't matter, he's dead."

We spent several hilarious sessions with His Silliness, Mr. Brooks, over the next few weeks. It was a master class in "What makes funny." The team reviewed *every Mel movie.* No single film lent itself to direct translation into a theme park attraction, but *Young Frankenstein* became our muse: silly *and* scary. We hit on the notion of a big, old, condemned, and humorously haunted hotel in old Hollywood—the Mel Brooks Hollywood Horror Hotel (original working title). As Mel often said, "Say 'Horror' slowly or it's no longer a family ride." To avoid that problem we nicknamed the project "Hotel Mel."

One day, during a round-robin storytelling session (each team member contributing, including Mel), we ruminated about a long walk (the attraction's queue line) through the gardens and lobby of a 1920s hotel, ending up in the basement steam room of this long-abandoned palazzo. We'd put guests in an old rusty elevator, lift them through several floors of special effects, then take the elevator off its track—*out of the shaft.* Running down the deserted halls of the decrepit art deco edifice, we'd crash into various rooms and "former" guests.

In the realm of WILD ideas, we had no way of knowing if unhinging an elevator was even feasible. I decided to interrupt the lunch of some longtime Imagineering engineers—guys who had worked on many Disney parks. This went against conventional wisdom: *Don't get the engineers involved too soon; they'll ruin it*—make it safe, slow, and boring. I thought they might want to play along. After all, they work at Imagineering, not Acme Freeway Off-Ramps, Inc. They had built a lot of fun, fast, not-at-all boring attractions.

I doodled the rough layout of the hotel (on a series of napkins, of course) and told the engineers our idea of going up past several haunted floors and then ... "out of the shaft and down the hall."

"Can we do that?" I asked one of them. "Can we take an elevator out of its shaft?"

"Sure," Jack said. He said it easy, as if I'd asked, "Can I have the pepper?" After several "yes" answers to many more wild, impossible questions, the engineers had a question or two for me.

Mainly they asked: "How will you get everyone back down to the lobby?"

I actually had an idea. The team hadn't thought that far. I was just hoping they wouldn't think I was nuts about taking an elevator out of its shaft. I had been using a salt shaker as the elevator and my floor plans on two or three dozen napkins as the hotel. "Well," I said, "what I'd like to do is crash through the outside wall of the hotel and ..." moving the salt shaker (elevator) to the edge of the table I released it and let it drop to the carpet. "I'd like to drop the elevator, *full of guests,* over the edge of the building."

... Silence.

"How many floors? How far do you want to drop them?"

"I dunno, six or eight stories."

"Nah," Jack—Disney Imagineering legend—said with a snarl. "Too short."

"Ten stories?" I said.

"Come on *Theme Park Boy*, think!" (Apparently the engineer thought I was the boring one.)

(Okay ... thinking ... it's the "Mel Brooks Hollywood *Horror* Hotel") "How about **thirteen** stories!"

"Good answer." Jack took another bite of his pastrami on rye.

As you read this it is several years after that fateful lunch—and Disney guests in Orlando, Anaheim, Tokyo, and Paris are falling MORE than thirteen stories in that "stupid idea" HATCHed over lunch in Glendale, California. The attraction is now called the *Twilight Zone Tower of Terror*.

I recommend that as often as possible, you ask a "stupid" question. Pursue the impossible.

Walt Disney said, "Never forget, it all started with a mouse." A *mouse*? What a *stupid* idea. Whenever I hear someone say, in a derogatory voice, "What a *Mickey Mouse* idea," I say, "Great! I'll take three."

[Illustration, above, by **Tim Kirk** who—along with his equally gifted brother, Steve—I invited to be on every project team I was asked to lead at Imagineering. Both Tim and Steve were on the first team I assembled that met with Mel Brooks, Michael Eisner, and our Imagineering boss, Marty Sklar. To my knowledge, Tim's drawing was the first rendering of "Mel Brooks Hollywood Horror Hotel" (a.k.a. "Hotel Mel" and now, "Tower of Terror") to imagine how it might rest at the end of the Sunset Boulevard expansion to Disney-MGM Studios (now Disney's Hollywood Studios), Walt Disney World. Drop in anytime.]

Deciding

After you practice Critical Thinking for a while, stand back and look at the three, four, or five groups of ideas that show some potential to become your Canada Invasion. If the team continues to return to one theme, one particular group of ideas, *that one* is your most likely answer. That's where everyone's imagination, energy, and enthusiasm are repeatedly being drawn. Use that inertia to carry over into HATCHing your planning and implementation stages to complete the project. The team's enthusiasm will also aid you in selling the concept to the rest of your company (especially top management).

What if we have three or four concepts we all like?

A great question and a *wonderful* problem! If you're using all *7 Agreements*, there is every reason to expect an outcome with MORE than one great concept. *Then how do we decide?*

Grab One and run a quick "pros and cons" exercise. Then repeat the process for each concept/theme. If you haven't already done so, this can be the time to introduce general budget and time constraints on the project that may commend the viability of one concept over all others. At the end of doing pros and cons on each theme, GRAB ONE that best withstands the test and get on with it.

A good question for this exercise, "What concept might lend itself to people remembering us (our company, product) best?"

Along with a pros and cons exercise, consider presenting each of the three top contending concepts to others in your organization who haven't been a part of the brainstorming team. Present them with equal enthusiasm (so as not to reveal the team's bias for one concept over another). Remember, though, these other folks are not voting on the outcome, but are serving as an in-house focus group.

If the project is large enough, it may well be worth the time, effort and expense to present two or three complete themes to actual focus groups of outside consumers. All they need to see is "Street Party," "Aerial Show," etc. No need to tell them it is the launch into Canada for your company. Brand names can often weight the opinions of focus group participants for or against the sponsoring organization. Make a generic or fictitious company with a similar product or service. You need a reaction to the launch event concept.

Once you choose your final concept/theme, take one last trip through your other Grouped ideas and themes to see if anything from them screams to be included in your ultimate plan. Brainstorming other solutions to the "invasion" can continue as long as you let it, but once you GRAB the big idea, keep GROWing in that direction and don't look back. Unlike brainstorming, planning and implementation of a project are *linear*.

The Mel Brooks project almost became Castle Frankensteen. In the pros and cons exercise there was much to commend a big, silly, scary, Old-World-Eastern-European village and haunted castle. BUT the castle had *no elevator*. Yes, and ... the old, deserted art deco hotel fit perfectly into the 1930s and 40s architectural theme of Disney-MGM Studios streets of old Hollywood.

[Later, during development of the big scary old hotel, a film buff at Imagineering recalled an old *Twilight Zone* episode involving an elevator. The clip was found, and it now serves as the opening of the preview film for guests in the queue area awaiting the next elevator—along with a voice over of someone imitating *Twilight Zone* creator Rod Serling to transition from the old TV clip into the *Tower of Terror* script.]

Onward and upward … and *downward*.

RECAP

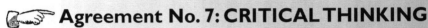 Agreement No. 7: CRITICAL THINKING

{Focused, purposeful, intentional thinking}

1. **GRAB**—Select a specific topic, from your thousands of ideas, to re-focus and focus your **Creative Thinking** on a theme for your Canada Invasion.
2. **GROUP**—Assemble all existing ideas (from your lists) that fit this new target topic and group them under the new header.
3. **GROW**—Brainstorm the NEW, more focused topic, adding to the ideas you already have Grouped together from earlier brainstorming.
4. **Repeat**—**Grab**, **Group**, and **Grow** (steps 1 to 3). Create at least **three** concepts. (Your themed launch for Canada Invasion.)
5. **Decide. (Get Moovin!)** Select one clear and certain concept/theme for the direction of your project and go for it.
6. **SAVE** all other themes you've developed to use for future projects. (More on this in the Storyboard chapter. Read on!)

"Put a pin in China, Herb."

Intermission

Gum
& Felt
Pens

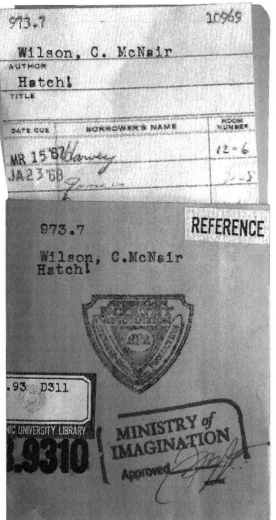

By now, you have thought of a couple of friends or co-workers who you know would enjoy reading HATCH! You will want to share your copy with them. DON'T DO IT !

If you loan this book to anyone, you will never see it again. They'll enjoy it and loan it to their friend ...and so on.

TRY THIS - Buy two copies for the people you think will most enjoy reading and using HATCH! Sign the book to them and write, "If you like this book, get a couple copies for your friends or co-workers. (See page 99.)"

Then, those two will each buy two books to pass on, and those four people will buy two books ...hey, it worked for AmWay.

Seriously. I give away copies of my favorite books which I used to loan and they NEVER came back.

The five senses are the ministers of the soul.

Leonardo da Vinci
Artist, Inventor, Scientist

YOU SHOULD HƎAR THE SMELL!
[*making scents of everything*]

"Imagine that!" What comes to mind when someone says that? Probably, an image—a picture in your mind. But Walt Disney encouraged (*expected*) Imagineers to engage in full-contact brainstorming when they began designing Disneyland—in the early 1950s—and create places that would appeal to *all five* senses—not just the look. (And at Disney, the *look* is huge. Key: Disney's level of *detail* in everything they design.)

Walt Disney said "imagination" suggests *image*—the way a place, object, or event *looks*. Walt never had a name for this all-senses design process. Mike Vance, founder of Disney University, called this process "Sensanation." I prefer easy-to-remember terms like *more* and *wild*. For Walt's all-senses process I use:

 ## Five Sensing

Try this: (With your brainstorming team) Write "**Christmas**" large, red, and fancy on the easel. Turn off all music, close all doors and windows to shut out any outside sound, and dim the lights. Try to achieve quiet. This is an exercise to teach "**Five Sensing**." Ask a short series of questions. No need to record the responses. This is to jump-start "Five Sensing." Say:

"What comes to mind? Don't say anything yet. Just imagine for a few moments." (Pause)
"What is the **SOUND** of Christmas?" Invite verbal responses from the team.

Bells, carolers, Mannheim Steamroller, crunching snow, laughter, Bing Crosby singing "White Christmas," crackling paper, children's choirs, Mariah Carey, Kenny G, and cash registers ringing ... "Bah! *Humbug!*"

As the group calls out auditory memories, repeat each one enthusiastically to affirm the contribution. Expect each person to have several impressions of the *sounds* of Christmas. Be sure to call on anyone who does not *chime* in.

"Great! And what is the **LOOK** of Christmas?" Red, green, Christmas trees, snow, twinkling lights, colorfully wrapped gifts, people bundled up in scarves and warm coats, more snow …

"What is the **SMELL** of Christmas?" Pine, cinnamon, cookies, baked ham, roast turkey, mulled wine, fresh-baked pies, bayberry candles, hot spicy cider … *mmmmore!*

"Yes, and … what is the **TASTE** of Christmas?" Cinnamon, cloves, hot cider, cookies, fruitcake, and eggnog! Exactly! If you are Presbyterian, eggnog with a little 'hmph' in it, right? For Catholics, it will be 'hmph' with a shot of eggnog. I'm Episcopalian, where we say, "Here's your Christmas punch. The eggnog is over there in the corner with the children's cookies. I just love tradition!"

"Finally, what is the **FEEL** of Christmas?" Cold, *and* warm, happy, stressed, surprised, anticipation, joy, celebration, cozy …

For each of the senses, cajole the team into calling out a sleigh-full of holiday memories and impressions. There are NO wrong responses. The last of the senses, FEEL, includes

tactile—cold weather, warm fires—as well as the *emotional* feel of heart-warming family gatherings, parties, and the anticipation of unwrapping presents.

Do you see why I like the simple, direct term "Five Sensing"? It is intended to make it clear to anyone as soon as you say it. At Imagineering we'd just say, "Put a little more Walt in it." Usually this meant more magic—elements of the unexpected. The enticing smell of baking cookies on Main Street, USA, *is* magic.

Since my first visit to Disneyland—age six—I have carried vivid memories of life-altering aromas emanating from the bakery on Main Street, USA, at Disneyland. My memories were confirmed decades later when a senior engineer at Imagineer told me the secret: Exhaust fans were in place from opening day—July 17, 1955—to blow aromas of fresh-baked goods from the ovens onto Main Street! Even architects and engineers were listening when Walt advocated engaging all five senses in design.

Five Sensing is a great exercise to jump-start the creative process while brainstorming on any subject from the Invasion of Canada to the company Christmas party. *Please* don't call it a "holiday party" or employees will also expect parties on Groundhog Day, Flag Day, Arbor Day, and the now-meaningless Presidents' Day (*Happy Birthday, President William Henry Harrison!*).

Making Scents at Work

What if you used Five Sensing, in your work spaces (offices, cubicles, lobby, lounges, break rooms, conference rooms, warehouses, and mail rooms)? Use this at home, places of worship, and retail spaces.

🕭 **Try this:** Close your eyes and imagine you are sitting in your office, cubicle, work space: How does it address—or completely ignore— **Five Sensing**? What is the **smell, sound, look, feel,** and even **taste** of your workspace. Taste? A bowl of mints or M&M's will do the trick. My Imagineering office had a gumball machine. (It's now in my guest bathroom—full of colorful push pins.)

What's the **LOOK** of your office? Bright, natural lighting from a window or skylight? Or, eye-scarring overhead fluorescents? Soft lamp light? What is your decor: colors, patterns, textures, artwork, books, mementos, and comfortable furniture? Typical office? (Are *you* typical?) Is your decor *you*? Maybe the look of your workspace came out of the head of some corporate interior design manager who developed all other work holes without regard to individual work styles or personalities. (I hope not.) What's unique or unusual about the contents, *arrangement*, and use of your space? What in your office does *not* look corporate or institutional? How many items with the company logo? (Check your scarf, tie, shirt, ball cap.) What about your office most reflects *you* and your personality? Any toys? Anything from your childhood?

What company office decorating guidelines have you "challenged" (or ignored) to make your office work best for you—in both function and comfort? If you enjoy working in your space and are productive there, you have a place that's yours. But if you find yourself regularly taking your laptop to the lunchroom, patio, rooftop, or across the street to *Rudy's Can't Fail Cafe*, then something needs changing—and it's not *you*. Stop reading—STOP!— dog-ear this page, and change your office **right now.** (It may require a visit to the warehouse of long-forgotten—and out-of-style—office furniture. The warehouse might only be a room, but EVERY company has one.)

SMELL :: What steps have you taken to control, adjust, and ensure pleasant fragrances in your workspace? Is fresh air available through a window? What can you do to enhance the fragrance in your office? Be aware, too, that strong fragrances may be enjoyable to you, but distracting to others. A little goes a long way. There is no such thing as a totally fragrance-free work environment. If you are more sensitive to fragrance use your creativity to invent ways to survive in a fragrance-rich world. Try spraying your curtains, rugs, and fabric chairs with Febreze®—available in light, natural scents. ("Curtains, McNair. I don't have curtains." Get some. I installed them in one office I had and I didn't even have a window!) Another aroma tip: Sprinkle a little dry carpet deodorizer at the end of your work day, before the custodial staff comes to vacuum. Invest in a small electric air purifier.

SOUND :: Do you control sounds and music in your office? Can it be silent, at least fairly quiet, or is there usually uncontrollable, distracting ambient noise from adjacent areas? If it harms your work product, pipe *up* and get it turned *down*. This may be a moot point as we seem to be becoming an iPod nation with our earbuds in place 8 to 5, daily—if not 24/7. Can you be productive without music filling your head all day? Try it for two hours, half a day …

> ⑤ **SpaceOddity** My offices have always had numerous available fragrances: pumpkin, vanilla, pine, and bayberry (scented candles, baked goods) along with sage and pinion incense from regular visits to Santa Fe. A giant, old, animation table (rescued from the warehouse of discarded Disney treasures) was home to recordings of virtually every musical genre. Lighting was always lamps and at least one window, however small. Overhead lighting tubes were removed. (If you can turn them off, someone will turn them on. I took them out.) :: It was the rare Imagineer whose work space was not a visual feast. There were toys everywhere—addressing our ubiquitous sense of play. Along with my toys, there were baseball caps rimming my walls, at ceiling height (more than one hundred). Most were gifts from friends returning from journeys 'round the globe. Some actually fit. And there was always a small plant or two and a small lamp to warm the place—to offset the overhead fluorescents if you work in a maze of cubicles. A small lamp, with just a 40-watt bulb, is worth ten degrees on the ambiance meter. Remember it's YOUR office.

During Creative Thinking, spend time imagining how your project (Canada Invasion) can and will appeal to all five senses. List *sensory* **goals**. How do you want people to feel as they experience this new product, marketing campaign, or facility redo? Create a sensory checklist. Set *emotional* goals as well.

Look at your three top concepts for the Canada Invasion. Take a deep breath. What do you smell?

When planning your organization's new offices, set sensory goals for common areas—especially the lobby (first impressions). Notice where you will need to add, change, or enhance aroma, temperature, decor, lighting, and other sensory cues. (**Smell** *is the strongest of the five senses associated with memory.*)

Imagine enhancements you can make by *five sensing* staff meeting areas, break rooms, conference rooms—all common spaces. We become accustomed to aromas in our offices—rarely noticing unpleasant, lingering odors until a thoughtful friend makes a helpful comment, a funny face, or runs out screaming and covering her nose. Take a field trip to discover how other businesses smell ... sound, look ...

Workplace aromas become familiar and "acceptable" to staff, but may be unpleasant to visitors. Air out your place on a regular basis, just in case. Your offices have an HVAC system: Heating, Ventilating, Air-Conditioning. Check with your facilities team to see if it is set to bring in fresh, *filtered* air. Many systems have that option, especially in rooms with no windows or ones that don't open. Ask, too, if your HVAC is on a regular maintenance schedule to check that it is fully functioning and filters are changed out or cleaned. This is also a health issue, which is a productivity issue.

Fresh air is invigorating. During lengthy brainstorming sessions (two hours or more) encourage everyone to get outside of the building for a bit. Weather permitting, grab an easel, a fist full of felt pens, and reconvene outside—even folding chairs in the parking lot or on the sidewalk. The odd locale will spark imaginations. Do not ask permission for any of this, they won't understand the question. Just go. I once moved a brainstorming session out onto the grass outside my Imagineering office. Security swooped in, "We don't think you can meet out here."

Looking around at my team I said, "Apparently we *can.*"

"We'll have to check and get back to you," they said.

They got back to me ... *two weeks* later.

Go outside!

We were given our five senses to enjoy all of life—full-body living. Do some full-body creating by *Five Sensing* all of your projects, work, and living spaces. Then invite me over!

OH, WHAT I'D GIVE FOR AN OPEN WINDOW

RECAP

 **Five Sensing**

- **Consider all Five Senses** (not just the LOOK) when planning events, designing new spaces, and remodeling work and public areas. Pay special attention to large shipping, manufacturing, and warehouse areas that use industrial materials.
- **Set SENSORY goals** for the project and how it will appeal to all five senses.
- **Set EMOTIONAL goals** for your project. What is the experience you want people to have? What can you build into the project to ensure those outcomes, consistently.
- **Apply FIVE SENSING** to your individual workspace—there's hope for cubicles.
- **Apply FIVE SENSING** to your home, car, garage work area, church, and club meeting hall.

THE AMAZING DONALDO

Every year at the all-company, all-night bowling bash, third-generation bowling ace Donnie Hulin—I.T. Special Projects Manager, Domestic—demonstrates his now-legendary "Tricks of the Lane."

Don's family owns Bowl-a-rama Lanes, where Don has worked since fifth grade. He installed the city's first computerized pin-changer; LED lights along all gutters; HD-interactive scoreboards; 5.1 surround-sound music system; automatic shoe refreshing machine (cleans & deodorizes in .6 seconds); and gourmet display kitchen, artisan bakery/pizza oven, and brewpub.

Following his bowling demo, Don signs autographs for the kids and enjoys a grilled bleu cheese burger (no pickles, no onions) and a Virgil's root beer—two if he's competing.

"Nature gives ME my BEST tools."

Salvador Dali, artist
(Known to have painted with
the tips of his five-inch mustache hairs)

Once Upon A Storyboard

[pinning it all down]

Every Sunday my local newspaper delivers a collection of colorful little stories told with words and pictures in simple framed scenes. Each frame, a moment in the lives of old friends: the feathered staff of the TreeTop Tattler newspaper in "Shoe," the dependably irreverent "Mother Goose & Grimm," the obstreperous "B.C." and his ancient neighbors, and so many others. The Sunday funnies, like their cousins the comic books (and more recently the high-concept, *graphic novel*), these are stories told in doodled snapshots. This is the happy heritage of the modern *storyboard*.

When Walt Disney and his animators broke new ground creating the world's first feature-length (83-minute) *animated* movie, *Snow White and the Seven Dwarfs (1937)* they used storyboards to translate the classic fairy tale from page to screen. Key moments of the story were drawn and pinned sequentially to large, bulletin boards, to build the story scene-by-scene. This process remains unchanged to this day—*seventy-five years* later. My friend Jay Ward at Pixar Studios, tells me that behind all their computer magic, storyboards were used on all of Pixar's miraculous, now-classic films: *The Incredibles*, *A Bug's Life*, all three *Toy Story* films, *Cars*, *Ratatouille*, *UP!*, *Brave* ('12), and the forthcoming *Monsters University* ('13), and *The Good Monster* ('14). Inside Pixar they refer to their story board sketches as "post cards from the future."

Long before computers join the process, every Pixar project is brought to life using storyboards with hundreds of *hand-drawn* scenes. Animators move their drawings, rearranging key moments, to build the story's sequences.

> ℘ **DO THIS:** Watch the documentary *The Pixar Story* (on Netflix, etc.). Along with the inspiration of this film, which follows the almost–accidental birth and growth of this creative powerhouse, you will see examples of their ubiquitous use of storyboards.

At Disney Imagineering we used storyboards frequently to design theme park attractions. Each card/sheet of paper on a storyboard illustrates a moment in the experience (the story) from the guests' point of view. (The best attractions, in *any* theme park, tell a story.) Many of our storyboards at Imagineering began as tiny "thumbnails" (drawings about the size of a business card). Selected ideas (from thumbnails) were redrawn (or enlarged on a photocopier) for use on a storyboard. Some storyboards began to take shape during critical thinking.

Live-action filmmakers caught on to storyboarding long ago for plotting scenes, planning camera angles, and preparing production schedules.

Orson Welles drew his own storyboards to devise his fabled first film—*Citizen Kane*. *Kane* is considered by film historians, critics, and industry professionals, to be the quintessential dramatic motion picture of all time. The *Citizen Kane* DVD contains examples of Welles' storyboards on which he planned his dramatic and exaggerated camera angles. James Cameron also drew many of his own storyboard scenes for *The Terminator*, *Titanic*, and *Avatar*.

Writers manipulate sentences, drag-and-drop paragraphs, and cut-and-paste chapters, just as animators and other filmmakers move scenes around on storyboards—long before filming or animating begins. Numerous computer applications for project management are set up like storyboards.

I used a remarkable writing program called Scrivener to edit much of this book—as well as my trusty and elegant Nisus Writer Pro—the best word processor on any platform. Scrivener software includes a storyboard tool that automatically turns any outline into an image of cards pinned to a corkboard. It's fun, facile, and endlessly useful. As you manipulate the cards, the text version of your project is automatically re-ordered in the same way.

Storyboarding is a bang-up medium to both communicate and track your plan visually to create and produce the "Canada Invasion" project with management, participants, and others. A thorough *planning* storyboard displays exactly what is in the works, how far along each element is in development, and what steps remain before completion.

Next you will see how to put all the ideas from your Critical Thinking sessions onto cards and arrange them in logical categories and progressions on the wall. Storyboard cards can contain just a few big words, a thumbnail drawing, or whatever visual cues work best to tell, step-by-step, the story of any project. Write details, if needed, on the back of each card. The face of storyboard cards can be as simple as: marching band, fireworks, parachutes, etc.

> ℑ **Storyboards** are most effective as a Critical Thinking tool—after the major pieces are agreed upon and Planning / Implementation begins. Some Creative Thinking coaches advocate Storyboarding during Creative Thinking. But I have found that trying to develop a linear Storyboard as you are also trying to create ideas will force people to think critically about the sequence rather than thinking creatively about raw ideas. Creative and Critical Thinking must always be separate activities. :: My preference for Creative Thinking is lists on easels or butcher paper on a wall—quickly capturing ALL ideas and making them visible to everyone, NOW. (WRITE BIG, so every thought is visible from anywhere in the room.)

Getting on the Boards

Once you choose a theme and direction for your Canada Invasion, begin building a *planning* storyboard. You can get a head start by writing each idea on its own (easily moved) card.

Use cards to create a bulletin board-size outline (story) for your invasion. The cards can be rearranged, added to, or deleted. Things change, or as my dad would say, "All of life is *Plan B*." As you begin building your Canada storyboard you will think of more ideas and add, subtract, and combine cards.

1. **Header and Sub-headers for a project.** The header for the entire storyboard reflects the final target topic or theme, e.g., *Total Domination of Canada*. Make your header **bold**—use a larger card or a sheet of paper and add color; make it hard to miss.

Make a sub-header card for each facet of the project (print campaign, parade, electronic media, product samples and giveaways, and everything else you've created). Sub-header cards serve as *chapter titles*—each a distinct category—telling the story of your Canada Invasion. Use standard index cards or recycled memos or other "blank-on-the-back" sheets of letter-sized paper (cut into quarters).

2. **Write every step** necessary to create the Canada launch on a separate index card. Create a storyboard to craft and distribute press releases, new product packaging, and so on. Every facet of the Canada launch should be laid out in a step-by-step storyboard. Allocating one step per card provides a flexible, changeable list. *Don't even try* to think of the steps in proper sequence—you will miss some. Write each step as it comes to mind: from writing and designing to photo shoots, graphics, printing, and mailing ... there are dozens of steps to creating printed materials. The same is true for the other operations necessary for crossing the St. Lawrence. Brainstorm every step necessary for each category of the project.

3. **Arrange cards (under sub-headers) in the order** that tasks will be done (left to right or top to bottom—your choice).

4. **Double-check lists** under each header (category) to identify steps that need to be added or rearranged. Any missing categories? Can any categories be *split* or *combined* to accomplish (and communicate) the task more effectively? Do not assume that everyone knows you need to request a check from accounting before you pick up posters at the printer. Make a storyboard card, "Get Check." Add cards as you think of steps. In many ways a storyboard is a giant, visual "To-Do List." It allows the entire team to track the project and communicate your progress with your entire organization.

5. Tell the world. (Start a fire, *again!*) For a big project like Canada Invasion, you will do well to post the primary project storyboard in a high-traffic area to enroll more participants from throughout your organization. It will also build enthusiasm for the event. Write the name of the department head or lead person on each *category header* and encourage people to contact them directly with ideas, time, talent, and additional resources.

6. Track and communicate progress. This is the main function of a storyboard. As each task is completed, turn that card over. Do not remove the cards or cross out the completed tasks. When all is accomplished, you can reuse cards with similar tasks for future storyboards.

7. Relax. (Everything doesn't have seven steps.) A lot of work has gone into getting the Canada launch out of your heads and hearts and onto the storyboard. Throw another log on the fire and enlist more participants to create a fully realized and successful launch.

The completion of storyboards can also be a good time to have a company meeting to present the project and steps (categories and sub-headers). Consider having the person serving as lead for each category present their steps so everyone learns whom to see to join that team. If you will be presenting your work to top management, I strongly recommend a dress rehearsal with the core team to refine the concept and tighten your presentation. Time and again I have seen good presentations sell projects with so-so concepts. Rehearse. Rehearse again!

Above All, Simplicity

Because a storyboard is a snapshot, it needn't contain every detail of a project. For *parade* there may be one card for marching band. The details for finding and hiring a marching band in each Canadian city can be listed in a project memo or on the back of the "marching band" card under the "parade" header.

Hold That Thought

Keep all the cards you create during Critical Thinking on all themes *not* used for your Canada launch. *Group* unused cards with a heavy-duty (long-lasting) rubber band. Label the top card: "Launch Ideas" or "New Country Launch." Save all these cards as they will be great kindling to re-ignite a fire for future themed projects. Throw them in a big envelope or an old cigar box marked "Australia Invasion."

For your next project :: Dig out all the unused idea cards, post them on a wall according to **GROUP** (parade, music festival, etc.). Then **GROW**, brainstorming each concept for the new project. Your not-yet-used idea cards form the beginning of your new Creative Thinking process. You are likely to have other launches for which the unused concepts from the Canada brainstorming might be appropriate. Add completely *new* themes, too. (Isn't it about time you thought about invading China, the UK, Brazil, Macedonia, or "(Company/Product Name) On the Moon."

You'll also generate cards that are interchangeable from one project to the next. All the cards telling the story of writing, designing, printing, preparing, and distributing posters can be used for a storyboard on *anything* that needs to be written, designed, prepared, and *printed*. Save those cards with a header "printed material." The steps to create an annual report will be 87.159 percent the same as for creating a brochure, poster, wall calendar, or catalogue.

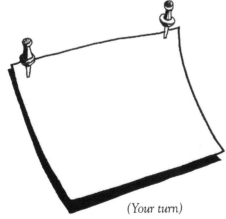

(Your turn)

Recap
👉 STORYBOARDING

- **Re-read** steps 1 through 7 for Storyboarding.
- **Do all steps**, especially No. 7.
- **Repeat** steps, frequently.*
- **Keep It Simple**. Storyboards are about story—beginning, middle, and end of the project. Details can be recorded elsewhere in longer documents or emails.
- **Communications and planning** are the main functions of a storyboard. (You are not trying to win the school bulletin board contest.) Have fun. Use colorful Sharpies, **bold letters** (**readable** from across the room), and the occasional doodle to communicate a concept visually.
- **Colored cards** can be used to differentiate between items that can be created in-house (blue), bought "off-the-shelf" (green), will require custom manufacturing (yellow), etc. Color communicates at-a-glance.

* If you get stuck while Critical Thinking deciding which of two or three competing concepts to use for a project, a quick and simple Storyboard can assist in deciding by laying out a completion strategy for each big concept (collection of ideas.)

"I've got to go lie down … and rest awhile."

I TOOK MY CURRENT JOB BECAUSE ALL THE GREAT SWORD SWALLOWING JOBS WERE ALREADY TAKEN

[Mini-poster for office, locker, or big rig dash: from HATCH! by C.McNair Wilson]

**Item No. 2 on my "To-Do" list:
"Get my priorities straight."**

McNair 3:27

"Lassie, get help!"

Timmy

Dr. Emile G. Sakowitz, inventor subconscious, inadvertent thinking.

PLAYING WELL WITH OTHƎRS
[finding the right people]

Push pins and felt pens and fruit plate and cookies ... bagels and schmear and hot tea with honey ... *these are a few of my favorite things.* These are the time-tested tools of brainstorming: snacks and art supplies. (Notice that phones, fax machines, laptops, Kindles, and iPads did **not** make the list—they are unnecessary distractions. *And take that hi-tech clothes pin out of your ear! They'll leave a message.*)

But the *first* ingredient for our brainstorming bouillabaisse is ...

 **People**

Getting the right people—building a team—is critical to the success of brainstorming. **Play** is the second essential ingredient of effective brainstorming. Playfulness is the key attitude required to remain open to all ideas, especially during Creative Thinking.

Even if you could assemble the five most creative people in your organization, that is no guarantee you will have the best outcome. If they lack a playful spirit and a willingness to work with others, all will be lost.

Brainstorming is a contact sport. While it's not cutthroat, brainstorming is challenging and should be executed with forceful attack. A strong **Facilitator** is the third essential ingredient—someone to serve as coach and referee. The facilitator must be able to function as a *full participant in the creative process*—with a few extra duties. The best facilitator brings a buoyant and encouraging presence—determined to get the most from everyone, but not dictatorial or condescending. She must be demanding in an "Oh, Boy!" way.

The facilitator is far more than the master of ceremonies moderating a conversation.

My composer friend Ken Medema and I collaborated on a musical that was performed ten times, daily, live at the World's Fair in Knoxville, Tennessee. The opening scene takes place in the legendary Garden of Eden (just outside Fallujah). After First Man and First Woman are evicted from the Garden they sing:

Too many gods will ruin the Garden.
Too many chefs will spoil the pot.
Too many chiefs and it turns into warfare.
Whatever made us believe we could be what we're not?

That's the challenge of creativity as a group process—*brainstorming*. It is not about chefs or bosses. No one person is "in charge" of the direction of the creative thinking or its outcome. Instead, the PROJECT is boss. The target topic sets the direction—generally at first and with more focus as you move into Critical Thinking. Brainstorming is meant to celebrate, savor, and capitalize on the boundless human imagination, life experiences, and individual brilliance of every team member. A person's spot on the company totem pole has no standing here. No one is Idea Boss. Every participant is of equal value in any brainstorming session. The facilitator's chief task is keeping everyone fully engaged and the process moving forward for the entire time allotted—to that last second.

The Odd Rule

An effective brainstorming team has three to seven people, max. (If Max isn't available, use Susan, she's amazing.) Why three? If you have only two people brainstorming (it *can* be done alone) you run the risk of creating "dueling ideas," degenerating to an impasse. Adding just *one* person (total of three) changes everything. Three is a more dynamic arrangement. (There's no such thing as a three-way tug-of-war.)

In several big projects I have been involved in, there were only three of us on the initial brainstorming team. Each of these projects became a major element of a theme park or major resort development. On those teams, most of our creative work was accomplished over long lunches or late dinners, away from the sandbox. (One was completed at Dodger Stadium, *during a game.*) On several such small team projects, all the brainstorming was written on dozens of napkins. As often as not, we were all writing and drawing simultaneously. (At Dodger Stadium, I took my sketchbook.)

Next time you're at Disney's Hollywood Studios (Walt Disney World), Florida, have lunch at the Backlot Express—between Star Tours and the Indiana Jones Epic Stunt Spectacular—and think of three Imagineering pals Bob Weis, Richard Vaughn, and me. As we envisioned what became that restaurant we enjoyed falafel, hummus, Mediterranean salad, gyros, lots of sparkling water, and tea. (I have not found alcohol improves brainstorming—in anyone.)

Is it *impossible* to brainstorm with only two? Certainly not, but it is faster and richer with three. Three heads are better (more dynamic) than two.

Why only seven, max? (I'm sure Max would concur with me on this.) Typically, when a brainstorming team has *more* than seven, some will *watch* while others *brainstorm*. Brainstorming is never a spectator sport. This is why we "start a fire" and get everyone thinking ahead of time.

Typically, *two* kinds of people emerge during Creative Thinking: *talkers* (external processors) and *people who think before they talk* (internal processors.) The facilitator should periodically stop and say, "Now, all the *talkers* be **silent** while we **listen** to _____ (indicating quieter "thinkers" *by name*) as they share the brilliance they've been storing in their heads the last few minutes. We know you're in there—time to come out and play." (Notice the words "silent" and "listen" both contain the same letters, rearranged. Hmm ...)

More than seven in a brainstorming circle makes it easy for thinkers to sit back and just think to themselves. (That's BLOCKING! Even in your head. Charge yourself one dollar.) Good ideas, tiny ideas, any ideas are for now, not later. Don't be selfish, speak up.

The Supreme Court Got It Right

The nine justices of the United States Supreme Court sit and discuss every case—after reading exhaustive (and exhausting) written briefs and hearing oral arguments. No one else is in the room for these discussions—not a secretary or court clerk. In these lengthy meetings, the junior associate justice (the most recent appointee to the bench) has a special place in the hierarchy. According to tradition, the "bottom of the bench" has the honor of taking notes, answering the telephone, opening the door, and pouring their colleagues' coffee during all private conferences. Justice Stephen Breyer spent ten years on the lowest rung, performing the court's grunt work—well into his late 60s. Once Breyer told that while serving coffee to Justice Antonin Scalia in 2005, he said, "I've been doing this for *ten years*. I've gotten pretty good at it, haven't I?" Scalia, who is infamous for exerting the court's most acerbic wit, shot back, "No, you haven't."
"I mean pour coffee," Breyer said.
"That too," said Scalia.
On every case they have a rule I have adopted on all brainstorming sessions I facilitate. I begin by going around the table and asking each team member to offer a few initial thoughts, impressions, ideas on the target topic—just a minute, or less. In the Supreme Court it is not a written rule, but it is a good one:

"No one speaks twice until everyone has spoken once."
As reported by Stephen Bryer, Associate Justice U. S. Supreme Court, 1994 - Present

This is a great custom to adopt when you begin Creative Thinking. It tells every team member—from the start—*your* ideas are welcomed here. Speak up!
Keep the size of your team small enough for all to interact, constantly. Call on specific "thinkers" to keep them interacting with the whole team. Thinkers tend not to speak up, but their silence does not signal a lack of ideas. If they're in the room, they have ideas. If everyone was notified in advance of the target topic, everyone *arrived* with ideas. (Frisk them at the door and check.) The entire team needs to hear ideas from both talkers and thinkers. When I assembled a team at Imagineering for a new project, some of my "must have" people were big-time thinkers. I always went to their office ahead of our first meeting and sat with them to *start a fire* in their head. In every case they arrived ready and were fully engaged.
The facilitator is also an active contributor of ideas—even a professional facilitator brought in from outside the company. Often a guest facilitator brings fresh eyes to your organization's current project—offering the point of view of your client or target customer. I am frequently hired to facilitate brainstorming from Creative through Critical Thinking

sessions, and I always participate fully. Not to do so would be selfish. Also, as an outsider my loyalties are only to the project, not to any department or administrator—even when I am hired by a longtime client or personal friend. I am there not to impress, but to improve the outcome.

But we've already invited eleven people ...

At this point in my seminars, a hand or two will shoot into the air and a voice begins asking, "What if you are in a small company, but there are eleven people? Is that too many for brainstorming? What should we do?"

My standard advice, professionally: "Since murder is probably not an option in your zip code, you will have to fire four people."

While many laugh, typically the questioner will jump back in, "No, really. What do we do?"

If you have a team larger than seven, maximize your brain power by starting with everyone together (all eleven) clarifying the target topic—*Canada Invasion*—and reviewing the **7 Agreements of Brainstorming** (having given everyone a copy of the book at least a week out). Then break into teams of seven or less to brainstorm. With eleven on staff, you could do three teams: four, four, and three.

This works, and I have done it—even in companies of a few dozen where management wants everyone in on the early Creative Thinking for a project that everyone, eventually, will be a part of developing. It is a powerful way to enroll the entire company or entire management team in the early creative work. It also builds enthusiasm for the project.

If you are dividing a large group into smaller teams, you will benefit from gathering the whole crew in one place to share ideas at regular intervals (twice a day). You can remix teams at any time to re-spark creative interaction. Consider meeting in a room large enough to allow Creative Thinking sub-groups to form in the same room, then regroup and report. (Reporting is a good way to maximize lunch time.) With multiple groups you will certainly come up with lots of different ideas. That's great. It maximizes your time.

Any outside guests? Yes! Consider adding a guest or two to your brainstorming. Your Canada Launch may require contributions and services from other professionals, making them natural brainstorming partners with your team. Consider including one or two longtime clients or customers. They will be honored by the invitation. Be sure to inform any non-employees that they will be asked to sign a non-compete, non-disclosure agreement. Find a way to protect your trade secrets and the product of your brainstorming and Critical Thinking sessions without shutting off the free flow of ideas from employees, consultants, and guests.

It is fair to pay guests for their time and to have a gift for outside participants, above and beyond their expenses. Most outsiders enjoy getting logo apparel or other items available only to employees. Such items have a value far beyond their actual cost. I have a closet full. I wear the ones that fit—or come in purple.

TakeNOTESMakeNOTES :: Inevitably, minds wander from the target topic. Here is a trick I developed for my own "off the path" imagining. Encourage everyone to keep scratch paper at the ready to jot down all ideas and side notes. When you are open to anything your mind will think of everything. During the Canada Invasion brainstorming, ideas will pop up for staff outings, break room decor, employee safety, etc. :: **Caution:** We all self-edit, deciding which of our ideas "fit the topic." We may be incorrect. From time to time, stop and ask for **side notes** to be read aloud. They will contain great, usable ideas and spur new thinking. I use my side notes to write down everything that comes to mind, while others are talking. Most often I share them at the first opening.

Priming the Pump

The facilitator always has an ice-breaker, brain-teaser, or riddle in her back pocket to jump-start gray matter at the beginning of every session. Here are four favorites:

- **Snapshot :** Ask everyone to compose a mental image of an ideal encounter they've witnessed with your product, service, or experience—then describe it as if it were a photo in an online album or scrapbook. For example: "Think back to our last convention and imagine you took a picture that made you think, *This is what we're all about.* Describe the photo. Who is in the frame? What are they doing? How do they feel? How do *you* feel when you see that?" Maybe it's a great idea you saw at another professional conference or convention you want to adapt.

- **Show & Tell :** One of my favorite ice-breakers is to ask each team member to bring a favorite memento from childhood for an old-fashioned "Show & Tell." This is good for the first session of the week so they have all weekend to rummage through their storage unit or their parents' garage. Remind them at the end of the last session of the week and send a short text message or email over the weekend. Each person tells why this item was a favorite as a kid, and why they still have it. This activity is great fun, insightful, and gets everyone talking freely. Leave all the Show & Tell items on the table to inspire your work together.

- **Invention :** Finish this sentence: "I wish there was a machine that ..." or, "Whatever happened to ..." (something that no longer exists, you want to bring it back), or "When's the last time you saw ...?" I have used all of these prompts, and more, as graffiti walls (on giant poster board with colorful felt pens hanging on strings) located in a high-traffic area of an office. It boosted morale and created creative interaction throughout the day.

WATCH AS I PULL A HAT OUT OF MY RABBIT

- **Magic Wand :** Give everyone a magic wand. Ask them to start waving it around, making spooky sounds. Facilitator: "When it's your turn, wave your wand and tell us one thing you will change in the category I will call out." As they begin waving their wands, point to someone and ask, *What will you change about your work space?* Point to another: *What one company policy would you change?* Point to another: *If you could live anywhere in the world for a year: where and why?*

Pushing

The key role of the facilitator is to keep the effort moving forward. A lull usually suggests that people are self-editing, self-blocking, and stuck in their heads. Silence does not mean that there are no more ideas left in the universe ... or the room. It's time for a great question to spur thinking. (See next chapter, *Great Questions*.)

"People! One Meeting, Please!"

A facilitator can be someone other than project leader, and the position can rotate among team members. But the facilitator must maintain "one meeting" at all times, during creative and critical thinking.

Allow no side conversations, whispered editorializing, secretive note-passing, or hallway and bathroom breakout sessions unless those ideas get shared with the rest of the team and added to the mix. Often the simplest thought, off-handed comment, or whim in our ever-wandering minds might be just the key to unlock a torrent of tasty ideas leading to the BIG IDEA.

"One meeting" keeps the focus on the target topic—be it hours, weeks, or months in the making. Halting side conversations is not about taking on the condescending attitude of "Substitute Teacher Hillary." When you say, "One meeting, please," it ensures that everyone hears every idea, thought, notion, and comment so they can be further inspired by even the smallest aside. Remind all participants to keep a note pad at hand to scribble and doodle any thoughts while others are talking so we do not lose *anything*.

Profile of a Facilitator

My father's well-worn, leather-bound *Webster's Collegiate Dictionary*, Fifth Edition (1941) defines **facilitate**: "to make easy or less difficult." Exactly!

The **7 Agreements of Brainstorming** are designed to assist the creative process in moving forward powerfully and productively. The facilitator acts as hall monitor throughout this process. But, that ain't all, folks. Other attributes of an effective facilitator include:

COACH Suggests new exercises or tactics, including pushing forward in an encouraging manner throughout the process. (Send us your ideas and we'll post them for others to benefit from on the Hatch-by-McNair-Wilson Facebook page.)

CHEERLEADER Enthusiastically affirms every contribution—tiny to huge—no matter the source. "Good, tell us more." As Cyrano would say, "You have your theme. Embroider it."

TIME–KEEPER Calls breaks. Assesses the best use of final minutes before lunch or day's end: "In our last fifteen minutes, let's have five more ideas from each person!" (There will be great ideas in those final minutes of exhaustion.)

NAVIGATOR Holds a steady course toward the target topic. Decides when the team should go down an unexplored path. (Rabbit holes can be exciting; just ask Alice.)

REFEREE Arbitrates all "Blocking" disputes and fines.

MINISTER Calms spirits and intercedes in arguments.

CAT WRANGLER Allows for wild, raucous, frenetic interplay, so long as it remains "one meeting" and no ideas are lost—no matter how wild or tiny. (A few minutes of playful chaos now and then can be as refreshing as a go-outside break.) "Everybody on your feet. Stand up! Now let's take three laps around the room, but keep talking." (Walking briskly.) Or … "Ed, get Sara some more tea, please."

INVESTMENT BANKER Determines what to do with all **Blocking Bowl** money—or allows team to decide. A frozen yogurt or ice cream run mid-afternoon is always a big hit. If your organization does lots of brainstorming, consider saving all blocking bowl funds for an annual event, our charity project (e.g., Habitat for Humanity), or a "Block Party" to celebrate when you've concluded brainstorming and are proceeding to implementation. All celebrations should include all support staff who enabled the process in any way.

RECAP

👉 PLAYING WELL WITH OTHERS

- **Assemble the Right PEOPLE:** the first critical ingredient to brainstorming.
- **An Attitude of PLAY** on the part of every participant comes next.
- **Begin** with everyone speaking for a minute on the target topic. Use "Supreme policy": "No one speaks twice until everyone speaks once."
- **Identify a FACILITATOR** to keep the process moving forward, discourage side conversations, call breaks, and be sure that **everyone** is participating (out loud).
- **Facilitator** leads an ice-breaker at the start of each session to jump-start minds. (The Facilitator may delegate this activity to a team member, but should give them at least a one-day head start.) The Facilitator can be other than the project leader, and the position can rotate among team members, or be an outside consultant. (Call me.)

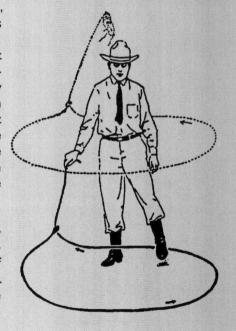

If you were assembling a Brainstorming team (of five to seven people) in your organization, make a list of some of the people you'd like to invite. (List at least ten names. You can have two groups two maximize the output.)

To be, or not to be: That is the Question.

Hamlet
HAMLET, Act III, Sc.1
William Shakespeare

GRƎAT QUESTIONS!
[add facilitator and stir]

CURIOSITY is the best friend Creativity ever had. Great facilitators ask great questions. Like water pouring over a wheel turning a millstone or the churning paddle-wheel propelling a grand riverboat up the Mississippi, Great Questions keep creativity moving. A well-placed "What if ..." or a timely "Why not?" can provide just the kick-in-the-corduroys your team needs to keep thinking. Facilitators develop an instinct for when to press on—and when to jump to another topic. Questions are essential tools.

Consider these two Great Questions:

What is it? What isn't it?

And beyond that, **What has it never been?** Or, **What should it never be?**

Asking what it's *not* is the time-honored detective's trick of narrowing the search by ruling out possibilities, eliminating suspects, weeding-out, editing, and thinning. Making a list of what it is not is always fun and stimulating—and can be quite revealing. It is a game of opposites: Not this, but might be *this*.

More Great Questions
{The words "this" and "it" refer to an idea, concept, project, etc. (e.g., Canada Invasion) }

• **What does this add or contribute to improve people's lives?**
Restructuring an entire company, a division, or redesigning a corporate image: Is it change for the sake of change—or is there a clear objective? Sometimes change for its own sake can be a good way to revitalize employees and customers. Get a new perspective by rearranging the furniture in your office, lobby, or family room. But other times, change can be a distraction—or a way to cover up a power grab or turf war.

• **What does IT want to be?**
A team member role-plays the topic, as if the project were a person you could talk to. Everyone conducts an interview. "Canada Invasion" might answer, "I want to be fun, exciting, silly, surprising, and unexpected!" Write down and elaborate on each attribute. Give each team member a turn in the interview *hot seat*. Each one might take on a different theme: circus ringmaster, military general, grand chef, space alien—all come to sell themselves.

- **Why? Why Not?**
The old "pros and cons" lists. Best used during Critical Thinking so blocking doesn't occur. The twist here: Everyone contributes reasons WHY they believe in this concept. After that rock is squeezed dry, the facilitator asks, "And WHY NOT?" What are the challenges of this idea? (*"I don't like it"* is *not* a challenge.)

- **What would YOU do?**
If it were all up to you, what sort of event would you like the Canada Invasion to be?

- **What have we never done before?**
(This is one of my favorite and most powerful questions.) Do NOT add blocking phrases, such as: …that we *can afford*, that we *know how to do*, that we are *allowed to do*, that would be *good, fun, profitable* or *easy to accomplish*. (See "Welcome to Camp Empty Lake," page 40.) Answer the question *as asked*: "What have we never done before?" Period. Go wild! What is the equivalent in your organization of **Donuts on the Moon**? (See Chapter 6.)

- **How can this be done simpler? Cheaper? Faster?**
What is possible without compromising project *objectives* or your organization's standards of excellence? A great target topic for an entire brainstorm is accomplishing your $7 million concept on a much smaller budget. Examine simpler systems, facilities, and organizational set-up for your entire operation.

Wild Questions

- **If FAILURE were not possible, what would you do?**
Inner critics are guaranteed to be right when you *choose* to believe them. My author and artist friend SARK recommends sending your inner critics on an assignment—feeding the starving in a far-off land. (She gives them one-way tickets!) I send my inner critics on a vital mission: "Sweep the Sahara!" Your "inner critic" is a product of your imagination, based on worry and fear. Use your powerful imagination to create powerful and productive alternatives. If you think you **can't** you will be right.

- **If the project budget were zero dollars, what would you do? Who would you ask to help?**
This requires your best thinking. It may include creating from existing materials and resources, borrowing, soliciting donations of goods and services, or recycling. Donations can also come in the form of asking your regular suppliers to give you the best deal ever in exchange for publicity for them in your campaign. (In the next chapter you will see examples of huge ideas accomplished on tiny budgets.) Consider "piggy-backing" your launch onto pre-existing events: Rather than staging your own parade (and all the government permits required), join a big parade already scheduled in each city.

• **If you didn't have to get anyone's approval, what would you do?** Usually this questions spurs WILD thinking that leads to great concepts. The facilitator reminds the team, "We are in charge here!" Great questions, *wild* questions can carry your team to great thinking and wild solutions (that will drive your competition nuts). Wild questions have the added benefit of making problem-solving fun. Participants will work together more playfully, harmoniously, faster, wilder, and want to apply the **7 Agreements of Brainstorming** throughout all areas of their work. Do it.

• **If you knew that coming to work would be fun, how might that affect your work product, punctuality, persistence, and daily interaction with coworkers? How can we make the workplace more enjoyable—more FUN?**
One of the best methods to encourage playfulness in the workplace is to encourage everyone to create more playful and enjoyable environments in their individual work space—office, cubicle, bullpen. This can even be done (I've seen it) in warehouses and factories. In industrial spaces there are certainly safety issues to observe, but they should not prevent playfulness. Think color, big graphics, music ... And make it a contest, with prizes.

Adding Questions

Keep a log to record new questions you develop that prove effective in sparking creative thinking (among all your various teams). Some companies keep a notebook—available to all—of exercises and other "games" they've used in previous sessions. Make a note, too, of which project a question or exercise was used on and what the better outcome was from that question.

Put a couple of participant names in your log so others can ask them for additional tips. (The next page can be copied and used to create a question catalogue for future Creative Thinking sessions.) Keep the "questions catalogue" in your company "sandbox" (creative thinking room.) See, "Build Your Own Sandbox" chapter.

RECAP

☞ GREAT QUESTIONS!

- **Great Questions Ignite** curiosity, imagination, invention, and productivity.
- **Break the Lull**: When things seem to be slowing or get quiet, ask a provocative question. (Unless a cattle prod is handy.)
- **GROW**: Brainstorm each question posed.
- **Shift the Conversation** to a new subject area when it seems the team has mined the current topic for every available gem. (You can add to or come back to any subject at any point.)
- **Creative Thinking is NON-linear.** Shift the topic to keep minds stimulated and everyone in the room engaged.
- **Play a Game**: Role-play an idea to flesh it out; make the idea a person and interview it.
- **Field Trip!** To research the "military invasion" concept, visit a military base, museum, or Army–Navy store to see the variety of equipment and vehicles available. Be sure to meet some paratroopers. Better yet, take the entire team skydiving! *

"We keep moving forward, opening new doors, and doing new things, because we are curious and curiosity keeps leading us down new paths."

Walt Disney

More Great Questions ...

(Use this page to record questions you develop to spur thinking in your own brainstorming.)

But what if our ideas are bigger than our budget? GREAT QUESTION! **Read on!**

**Ask and it will be given to you.
Search and you will find.
Knock and the door will be opened for you.**

Jesus
St. Matthew's Gospel
Chapter 7, verse 7
(J.B. Phillips, New Testament)

SMALL BUDGƎT, BIG NOSE, LOUD TRAIN

[The train left at 9:25 p.m., his nose left at 9:12]

At Walt Disney Imagineering, every project had an unlimited budget. We could design and build whatever we wanted and take as long as we liked to get it done. Disney management gave us as much money as we requested and when we ran out, they gave us lots more. Cost was no object.

BULL-*loney!*

Even the largest budgets have limits. May you never be "blessed" with a half-billion-dollar budget. Disney Hollywood Studios budget toward opening day was $600 million. We spent every dime, accounted for every penny, and worked more hours than we recorded on our weekly time sheets. (Before opening day we began work on concepts and designs for the next phase of that theme park and working studio.)

The only difference between your budget and any budget at Disney, Universal Studios, Apple, etc., is that on those huge projects there are 187 people looking over your shoulders (armed with calculators) checking every dime spent and every line drawn. Every Imagineer, every week, had to turn in a detailed time sheet accounting for every minute of our lives—except lunch and potty breaks. Every project had a phalanx of bean-counters.

One such Disney money-monitor (at EPCOT Center), who became a friend, once boasted, "I am not merely a bean-counter, sir. Oh, no, my friend. I am a bean-sorter, bean-purchaser, bean-cataloguer, bean-watchman and (with sweeping gesture and pen in hand) bean-historian!"

More importantly, Tommy saw himself as a partner in the creative process. He was right; we could *not* have done it without him. He was the king of business managers. If you asked him, "How much is two plus two?" Tommy would say, with a straight face, "How much do you need it to be?" Good answer!

When it came to dreaming up new theme parks, our right brains were always bigger than Mickey's wallet. I worked on six new Disney parks, two new resort entertainment complexes, and several new attractions for existing parks—all from scratch. By the time each was built, every one of those projects was greatly reduced in scope and scale from the original "approved" concepts.

"What happens when the ideas we create are bigger than our budget?" I thought you'd never ask. If you really think about that question, you **always** want that to be true, because the reverse is worse: A small idea with a big budget will produce a big mess. How can your big ideas be squeezed into your too-small budgets? Use the **7 Agreements of Brainstorming** to create ways to do more (better) with less.

Consider the following real-life adventure. (This is a true story—I was there for it all.)

"If money is your only problem, you don't have any problems!"

C. Elwood Wilson (my dad) . . . who had little money and few problems

A Midsummer Night's Scheme
(A miracle in five creative acts)

Backstory

Scene: Dinner party
Place: "In fair Pasadena, where we lay our scene ..."
Time: Spring, 1991
Cast: Professionals in film, television, theatre, visual arts, and other media
Prologue: Our host, who knew everyone, wanted us all to meet. Most of us were meeting each other for the first time. One of the guests had a big idea—huge. Eric had long dreamed of creating a summer theatre program to mentor teenagers by producing fully staged productions of classic plays—the sort that employ rich language and grapple with moral and ethical issues. The mentoring would be on life issues and rehearsals would include training in the basic disciplines of theatre arts. Virtually everyone at this dinner said, "Count me in." (Even spouses who were not actively engaged in the arts.)

Act I

"In fair Verona, where we lay our scene ..."

Spring 1992. One year after that dinner party we began auditions for the premiere production of Theatre Quest (TQ), just two weeks after riots shook Los Angeles following the verdict in the first Rodney King trial. Eric and producer Lauralee, assembled a group of professional actors, designers, and a legion of area teenagers. We gathered in Pasadena High School's 1,200-seat auditorium to rehearse and present William Shakespeare's *Romeo and Juliet.* I was invited to inhabit the role and burlap cassock of Friar Lawrence, priest, herbalist, and family friend.

Our poster (right) carried the title in swirling calligraphy beneath a photo of a nineteen-year-old Asian-American "Romeo" and a nineteen-year-old African-American "Juliet." This striking black-and-white poster was sent out with a press release that began with the play's opening lines:

Two households, both alike in dignity ...
From ancient grudge break to new mutiny.

The *Los Angeles Times* placed the photo of our "two star-crossed lovers" in the center of an editorial observing that corporate and governmental do-gooders merely organized committees and press conferences to placate racial tensions. Meanwhile, off in Pasadena, a quiet army of artisans and teenagers was actually bringing the races together for a common good. Good theatre—in the form of a rousing and lyrical discussion on prejudice, albeit in verse. But such verse!

The *L.A. Times* editorial, word-of-mouth, and other media attention brought an audience unlike any I have experienced in my four decades on stage—elementary kids clutching autograph books, senior citizens in their best evening attire, Gen-Xers in jams and flip-flops, and moms and dads in fancy dress, and ties—all to see and hear the Bard: Shakespeare!

Our on-stage cast was forty-four people! (That's enormous by modern theatre standards.) The costumes, lights, makeup, and poster and program design and printing were all donated. Not one syllable of Shakespeare's four hundred-year-old script was altered or simplified. Even so, we never had to explain to teenagers what it all meant—not the feuding families, young love, and especially not the twin suicides. Every teen in the cast knew someone who had committed suicide, attempted it, or thought about it—including members of our acting company.

In spite of the large proscenium stage we rehearsed on, our scenic designer envisioned a "fore-stage" to thrust the story forward, into our audience's lap. This would require lots of good, sturdy lumber.

The agreement among all participants was that everyone worked for free—no gas money, makeup stipend, not one cent. We all agreed—professional artists to teens—crossed our fingers, said a prayer (lots of them) and proceeded believing something good was about to happen. Theatre Quest's first summer exceeded our hopes in every area of the project.

In the first week of rehearsal, while running errands with students one Saturday, our producer passed a lumber yard. They stopped, told the owner about TQ and showed him the plans for the large stage addition.

"I saw your picture in the paper," he said.

"Our plan," they said, "is to ask area lumber yards to donate scraps or whatever they can spare."

Studying the blueprint more closely, he said, "Let me tell you a story."

"We're kinda in a hurry."

"You'll like this story." When his daughter was in high school, she almost died of a drug overdose. She had been involved in theatre at her school. Those drama kids turned out to be good kids—the only non-family members who visited her in the hospital. Later they helped her get her life back together—drug free. A drama major in college, she was now teaching theatre back East.

By now he was a little choked up, but he continued. "I've been waiting almost twenty years to find a way to thank theatre people for giving me back my daughter. You're the ones. Take all the lumber you need—and from the front of the yard, the good stuff. Send your designer over and my guys will deliver it."

We just asked the right question of the right guy.

Most people never even ask. They don't make their needs known to those who can assist with goods, services, experiences, contacts, expertise, or hands-on help. Sometimes you can even get a bigger budget (if you have "more pirates" or summer camp cabins with giant animal heads). Ask.

Theatre Quest became emboldened about asking, publishing a list of everything we needed and sending it home with every cast and crew member. Goods, services, and contacts flooded in.

Beautiful costumes were lent by large college theatre departments, movie studios, and NBC television—all for free. Professional costumers from big studios brought seamstresses, professional sewing machines, and bolts of luxurious fabrics to make or mend lavish period costumes. They were all friends of friends of somebody connected with the vision of TQ.

Romeo & Juliet was a roaring success, theatrically and in the lives of the participants—young and old—and audiences that grew every night.

Act II

de Bergerac

Paris in the Park
Old Pasadena, California, 1993

The following summer we planned a grand outdoor production of the swashbuckling romantic comedy, *Cyrano de Bergerac* (bair' zhuh raak.) I was invited to be director of an on-stage cast of—wait for it—sixty-six actors. They ranged from a seven-year-old boy with a challenging speech impediment to a battalion of enthusiastic and talented teens, collegians, adult actors from area community theatres, and a core of professional actors in the four critical leading roles. Again, everyone worked for free, a Theatre Quest policy on all levels for every production.

Let There be Light

Cyrano's theatrical home was the amphitheater and band shell in Old Pasadena's Memorial Park. One afternoon, a father noticed we had no stage lighting—worse yet, we had no place to hang lights even if we had them.

One night this big, take-no-prisoners dad stood with me and asked, "Okay, Mr. Director, where do you want your lights?"

"There's nothing here but sky." I pointed straight up.

"Humor me," he pushed. "Dream a little, Mr. DeMille."

"Here, Mr. Bower. Right above where we're standing. But where are you going to—"

"Look." Pointed into the trees surrounding the seating area. "Do you see what I see?"

With my best Stan Laurel smile I said, "Yes I do, Ollie."

"Leave it to me, Stanley." He poked me on the chest.

He was just a parent picking up his three kids from rehearsal. The following Saturday he returned with a forty-foot steel lighting truss he had built at home—in two pieces. We were met at the amphitheater by two City of Pasadena trucks with crews and hydraulic lifts. What Dave had pointed out to me in the trees the week before were four steel towers—which is where the crew proceeded to stretch City of Pasadena cable, hanging Theatre Quest's new lighting truss in mid-air. Right where I had pointed!

"How did you get these guys to ..."

"I know a guy. I made a couple of calls." Tony Soprano has nothin' on my friend Dave Bower.

The sky is NOT the limit—not for my friend, Mr. B—not for you, not ever!

For all I know, that lighting truss is still there. Come to find out, Dave had an engineering degree from a little college in Pasadena called Cal Tech; you may have heard of it. When he asked me, "Where do you want your lights?" I pointed.

Dave (and the City of Pasadena) did the rest.

Act III

Who Nose What Cyrano Might Have Cost

We mounted these huge productions for virtually nothing—very little cash outlay in advance. If I had been paid for being director, plus the going base rate for our four principle professional actors, costumer, seamstresses, costume rental, photographer, graphic designer, PR agent, producer, printing costs, ticket agency fees, amphitheater rental, lighting equipment rental, plus a small stipend to a dozen semi-pros, et al., *Cyrano* could easily have cost $140,000 to mount. At that price, it would have been a bargain. But Theatre Quest's *Cyrano*—with a cast of sixty-six and a backstage crew of three dozen at every performance—cost about $5,000 in actual cash outlay—for paint, spare buttons, etc. But the creativity contributed by everyone involved? Priceless.

Cyrano's nose was custom-made by one of the top makeup artists from one of the busiest special effects companies in Hollywood. They made enough noses so that Eric (Cyrano) had a fresh nose for every performance— including several rehearsal noses.

Cyrano's enormous hat and plume were also custom-made by one of the oldest hat makers in Hollywood (actually, Burbank). Everywhere we

(Poster photo by Carrie Mooneyham:
Eric de Waterhouse as **Cyrano de Bergerac**)

turned there were costumers, stage fight directors, bakers, carpenters, and a legion of parents who wanted in on the TQ MAGIC. Panache!

Act IV

Cyrano vs. Amtrak

We faced one minor glitch producing *Cyrano de Bergerac* that no amount of money could have overcome. It was the most intriguing challenge I have ever encountered as a theatrical director—the ultimate immovable object—the National Railroad Passenger Corporation—a.k.a. Amtrak.

Thirty paces from the amphitheater stage lay the tracks of the Southern Pacific Railroad. Every night at 9:10, Amtrak's Southwest Chief train pulled into Pasadena's Union Station, one mile down the track from Memorial Park. At or about 9:35, it rumbled, roared, grunted, and screamed through Memorial Park on its way to "Winslow, Albuquerque, Kansas City, and Chicago-o-o-o!"—threatening more than a little distraction for our nightly live performances.

Cyrano de Bergerac was written as a five-act play. We planned to present it in two sections with one intermission. I believed we could perform the first half in a brisk ninety minutes (curtain time: 8 p.m.). We kept pushing the pace of rehearsals toward that goal. Weeks before opening night, our printed program had to go to press. Knowing we might have a train running through the scene that closed our first half, the producer and I placed a line in the program: "There will be one fifteen-minute intermission, or until the 9:35 to Santa Fe rolls by."

My producer ask, "Can we do it?"

I said, "I think we can, I think we can ..."

The trick would be to keep scenes moving at a brisk, swashbuckling pace—especially the more comedic moments.

The cast was more nervous than usual for a big production: The first half ends with a secret marriage between Christian and Roxanne, angering the villainous Compte de Guiche—himself in love with Roxanne (aren't we all?). The vengeful de Guiche reverses his orders and announces that he will send Cyrano, Christian, and the entire Gascon regiment to war. Punishment and revenge with the stroke of his feathered pen.

As they march to war, Tom Howard's heroic original score (written for this production) swells, "Sound the assembly!" A live drummer appears on stage. Gascon soldiers with wives, children, and girlfriends rush in from everywhere, even down the aisles (kicking up just

Memorial Park
Pasadena, CA

< Amtrak tracks (Left side)

< Existing band shell/ stage

< Old towers to which new cables were attached by city workers

< New lighting truss suspended on cables

< Rows of benches on sandy area inside tree lines

< Tech booth, lighting control

enough Pasadena dust for excitement). They all hurry off, stage right, in the direction of the train tracks. This was one of the four scenes in which all sixty-six cast members appeared onstage.

At dress rehearsal, three nights before opening night—in the midst of all the running, frenetic farewells, soaring music, drumming, and cheering Parisians—the federal government of the United States of America disguised as a passenger train, entered, stage right, with the biggest and best special effect that ever rumbled, roared, grunted, and screamed through a live play anytime in the history of the American theatre.

The first time it worked in rehearsal was thrilling. The cast came running back on stage cheering and laughing.

"Will that work every night?"

"It's up to us to make it happen." I said. "The train won't miss its cue and neither shall we!"

And so we did! Audiences were stunned—every night. Intermission began with gales of laughter and thunderous applause for the cameo appearance of one big, loud, honkin' train.

"How did you do that?!" Many audience members asked at every performance.

Most impressed were the scores of theatrical and film industry professionals who were drawn to Theatre Quest performances—including many recognizable celebrities.

Never accept "NO" or "Amtrak" as an excuse for not accomplishing your creative goals.

OF COURSE you'll face budgetary and other challenges. Every project faces these challenges. Make a plan. Work your plan. Adjust, fix, and change the plan. Brainstorm! Press on. Move forward ... don't let the idea train leave without you.

Life is not about removing every obstacle; it is about finding creative solutions for taking advantage of those obstacles, or learning from them ... or living *with* them.

"The Gettysburg Address" was quite short because President Lincoln was informed he would not be the main speaker that day (November 19, 1863) for the dedication of the battlefield cemetery. Thus he would have a short time (obstacle) to "say a few words." What if he had refused to attend given such a short time to speak? He saw the occasion as important and chose to maximize the moment. Abraham Lincoln spoke only 269 words that day.

We're still saying them.

Act V

A Capital Idea, Summer 1995

The Kennedy Center in Washington, D.C., invited Theatre Quest to produce *Romeo & Juliet* on the stage of their largest venue, the Opera House. The Washington Opera donated costumes and sets from their production of *Rigoletto*. TQ mustered a company of adult and teen actors representing the rainbow age and ethnic flavoring of Pasadena and inner-city Washington. The production was huge—and so was the reaction of all Washington. Many of the families of teens who participated in the production, though they lived only a short distance from the Kennedy Center, had never been inside "America's National Cultural Center."

All this—five productions in four years—was the fruit of a small dinner party with friends where one of those friends shared a dream—an idea—and the rest of us said, "**YES, and ...**" here's what I can add to that idea.

"Shall I build my reputation on one flawless poem and never write another, should I scheme to get my name mentioned in the columns of some newspaper and smack my lips over little praises written about me? No, thank you!"

Cyrano Hercule Savinien de Bergerac
French Poet & Swordsman (1619-1655)

Recap
☞ BIG IDEAS
Small Budgets
(Tiny Budgets)

When the final outcome of a Brainstorming session is far grander than the resources available to execute the project, use the **7 Agreements of Brainstorming** to inventively attack budgetary, scheduling, and other challenges.

In fact, be certain you ALWAYS create ideas that are **bigger** than your budget. The opposite is death: sinking too much money to produce weak, ordinary, small ideas.

Try this:
- **Brainstorm budget, resource, and scheduling issues**—just as you did the concept.
- **Create a budgetary storyboard** and post it in a high-traffic area to collect ideas and resources from other staff members.
- **Brainstorm** with money people, tech heads, project managers, and production specialists, procurement teams (a.k.a. "finders"), and other specialists in your organization. (Bean-counters have imaginations, too.)
- **Publish a NEEDS LIST** of goods and services required for the project.
  - Place the list in pay envelopes and on bulletin boards.
  - Make table tents of your list for break rooms and eating areas.
  - Include the list in company publications, employee newsletters, and intranet communiques. ("Needs" include personnel, vendor contacts, and other resources not readily available in-house: "Does anyone know **anybody** in Canada?"

Don't forget:
- **A good amount of inventive budgeting** can come from rethinking the original concept. How might we accomplish our objectives and goals more efficiently and effectively, in terms of time, resources, and staffing? Remember my friends in Texas at The W!LD Summer camp: they worked with both the vendor who was fabricating the giant animal head cabin facades and the camps board to come to a financial compromise.

There is nothing in a caterpillar that tells you it's going to be a butterfly.

Buckminster Fuller
Inventor of the geodesic dome

::

BUILDING YOUЯ OWN SANDBOX

[be sure the felt pens work in advance]

WHERE we brainstorm can affect HOW we brainstorm and WHAT we create. Don't get me wrong: I don't think place is as important as people (see previous chapter)—but I do think a great space brings out the best in people. If you're lucky, you'll have the resources (space, time, and budget) to "build" your own creative sandbox. To succeed, you will need more than a conference room with a coffee can full of felt pens and a stack of index cards. A few guidelines:

 **[The Facility]**

General Considerations

"Sandbox" was my nickname for Disney Imagineering. I later learned, from some longtime Imagineers (who designed Disneyland) that Walt Disney called Imagineering his sandbox. He thought of it as a place to play with his ideas and bring them to life.

Make your Brainstorming space visually stimulating. Encourage team members to bring photos, posters, magazine clippings, doodles, newspaper headlines—even three-dimensional props and other eye candy to post on the walls or place on the table to play with and stimulate imaginations. These items may change according to the project at hand. Many of my regular clients keep permanent "toy boxes" in their sandbox/think tank.

IMS Productions (film production), a longtime client, along with boxes of toys in their brainstorming room, had a secret passageway from the president's office to their sandbox. All clients entered the space via that "tunnel"—complete with special lighting and sound effects. (I used it coming and going.)

Words have meaning. So spend a bit of creative thinking time deciding what to call your brainstorming place. A favorite, very creative client of mine mysteriously calls theirs the "war room." Argh! Unless you are in the military and your brainstorming room is in the Pentagon (or a tent in Fallujah, Iraq) do not use "war room." Creativity is not a battle or a brawl. The problem is that brainstorming *has* been fighting and bickering for too long. The **7 Agreements of Brainstorming** puts an end to that. Call your creativity thinking space something easy and obvious. I called any room I worked in at Imagineering the (name of project) sandbox. Use that. Or ... think tank, idea factory, brain room, play room, the cloud … Would you rather be invited to spend a day in one of those places or the "war room"? Even *creativity cave* is better. A pastor friend had an Imagination Station—*great.*

The phrase "room temperature" was coined regarding the decanting of red wine in the brisk and chilly, stone-walled environs of French chateaus and Italian villas, not today's over-heated restaurants. (Hence, most red wine today is served too warm!) Theaters, auditoriums, wine cellars, and brainstorming rooms are best kept cooler rather than warmer—for the benefit of what happens there. A warm place is not a creating place. Warm rooms make people lethargic, overly comfortable, sleepy, and unproductive. If you regularly keep the room cool (not cold), people will learn to bring sweaters if they need them. (Keep a small stack of "brainstorming blankets" handy.)

Encourage your company store to stock medium-weight "Creative Thinking apparel"—year round:

I Think
Therefore I'm Cold

§

I'm Not Cold, I'm Imagining

§

Brainstorming is Cool!

The most effective brainstorming rooms feature floor-to-ceiling, pin-able surfaces (available at fine home-supply depots everywhere). At least have walls on which you may tape anything. Stock up on *low adhesion*, "low tack," drafting tape (a.k.a. painter's tape). Camps and non-urban conference centers offer ideal locations for this purpose, if only for a day away. (Most church camps rent meeting rooms by the day and can usually prepare a hearty lunch.) Hotel "conferences rooms" are the worst. ("Please DO NOT put anything on the walls. Lunch will be $47.85 per person. Coffee is half that—*more*, if you want real cream.")

I have worked with several companies that had numerous rooms equipped for brainstorming, but we still held frequent off-sites. Even in the best work environment, a change of scenery can stimulate creativity.

For the Disney project that was being planned for the waterfront in Long Beach, California, I held early Creative Thinking sessions in the luxurious old Captain's Dining Room aboard H.M.S. Queen Mary. I showed up the first day in my father's U.S. Navy uniform—he was a full Commander.

This project, as originally slated, would have included the H. M. S. Queen Mary and the "Spruce Goose" Howard Hughes' giant plywood aircraft. It was eventually expanded (*Yes, and …*) and built in Japan as *Tokyo DisneySea* theme park, next to Tokyo Disneyland. Good ideas are not lost, if you save them.

White Board Malfunction

Over the years, and thousands of hours of brainstorming, I have developed a strong preference for large paper pads on easels rather than erasable white boards (with their disappearing ideas). With paper, nothing is lost. We can refer to our lists throughout the days and and weeks of brainstorming. Staring at the walls we may rediscover a yet-to-be-developed gem from our lists of ideas. White boards must be recopied, erased, and started over. I've tried them all—even the white boards that make printed photocopies of themselves. Clever but tedious.

The Case Against White Boards :: When white boards are used, they fill up. They must be erased to add more ideas. My experience—over, and over, and over again—is that just before erasing a white board someone asks, "Anything here we want to save?"

THAT is Critical Thinking, and, as you know, that comes *later*. Now is not the time for us to turn off our creative juices and figure out which ideas we may need, want, or use later. We can not know that. We need all ideas saved and posted in plain sight. This point in the process (during Creative Thinking) is not the time to decide anything.

Burn your white board. It is your enemy. (Or cover it with white butcher paper!)

When using large pads on easels, tear off each full sheet and tape or pin it on the wall for constant reference. (No need to flip back and forth.) Write the subject or target topic at the top of **every sheet**. Consider using the easel-sized Post-It style note pads; they work nicely and can be removed or repositioned often. Use big pads. You want to capture every thought, quickly and visibly. Write big enough to be readable from across the room.

Eliminate distractions. Getting away from phones, pagers, faxes, laptops, and any other gadgetry that connects to WiFi—any source of interruptions and distractions—will assist your team in unleashing their creative spirits. Scheduling a session off site will send a signal about the importance of the project. When you do this, tell no one where you are for the day! Set cell phones and other communicators on *silent* or stow them away until lunchtime. One VP at a client that creates custom parts for NASA passed a bread basket around the room and collected pagers, cell phones, CrackBerry devices, etc.—and took them out of the room to a drawer in a nearby staffer's desk. There was grousing, at first, but it helped focus the team for the all-day creative sessions. Most of us lived and worked for years without these annoying WMDs (Wonders of Mass Distraction); we can survive until lunch without our electronic leashes.

"A desk is a dangerous place from which to view the world."

John Le Carre
Writer, tinker, novelist, spy

Tell everyone at the office, "I'm taking a sick day." (Sick of phones, sick of interruptions.)

Building Your Own Sandbox

Caution: Outfitting your own dedicated "sandbox" (Brainstorming Room) is not necessary to do world-class Creative Thinking. But enhanced environments do stimulate creativity, even with modest resources.

Having assisted numerous organizations (including many non-profits) in designing and creating on-site, dedicated, think tanks, I have developed two lists for assembling a company sandbox—a place to play, imagine, and *create*. Once this place exists, you will find yourself going there just to think creatively—alone—even when it is not being used by a brainstorming team.

Must Have Elements:

Whether this is to be a permanent place or just a temporary transformation of a conference room, here are the essential ingredients for optimizing brainstorming (and where to find these simple tools).

- Check and restock all **ART & OFFICE SUPPLIES** frequently. There's nothing more frustrating than a room full of ideas and nothing but dried-up markers. (Double-check and refresh supplies before EVERY session. Buy TWO of everything.)
- "JUMBO" FELT PENS for words/doodles on easels—as many colors as you can rustle up and two or three of each. If the room is not well-ventilated, use water-based markers. Always write with strong colors and PRINT big so everything can be seen from anywhere in the room. Use green, blue, red, brown, purple, and black (if you must). If you find jumbo markers in purple, buy a box for me. Use orange, or yellow ONLY as highlighters as these colors are difficult to read from across most rooms. ["Jumbo" maker source: Art or office supply stores]
- TWO EASELS, minimum—(Four-legged easels only) with large, UNLINED PADS—Post-it® style pads are great for easy wall placement. [Source: Office supply]
- Buckets filled with small, water-based (fragrance-free), writing size **COLORFUL FELT PENS** for note taking and storyboard cards. Encourage everyone to use colored pens

(NOT ball point) for ALL writing and note taking. (They will think differently. See chapter 14: "The Doodle Factor") [Source: Drug stores, Target, and Walmart all sell packs of fifty different colors for well under $10.]

• Crate of **PUSH PINS** to attach doodles, magazine pages, storyboard cards to wall or bulletin boards. [Source: Art or office supply stores]

• One billion **INDEX CARDS** (3x5) for storyboards, (Recycled memos—blank backside of anything—can be quartered and used just as effectively as index cards.)

• "Medium or low tack" **MASKING TAPE** (also called "drafting tape") for posting doodles, photos, posters, and other visual inspirations. Drafting tape won't harm wallpaper or paint. [Source: Art, office, home repair supply stores]

• **LARGE TABLE** for sitting and working together. You may want to "build" something big enough to accommodate lots of room to work on big projects. [Source: Used office furniture warehouse. Many city governments sell surplus office furniture and school stuff. Make a call. Habitat for Humanity may have a "ReStore" salvage shop in your community.]

• Low **CABINET** (so as not to block wall space) to store and lock extra supplies.

• Comfortable **CHAIRS** that swivel to face any direction.

• Basket full of **TOYS**, puzzles, balloons, blocks, beach balls (for inspiration). When your team's creative thinking slows, the facilitator tosses out a beach ball or balloon (or three) to distract thinking for a bit. It will spur many more ideas. Try it!

• Space for an additional table or rolling **CART** for food, ice bowl, beverages, snacks, etc.

• Enough **ROOM** to get up and pace, paste, and post—and break into smaller teams

• **Phone with no ringer** to "call so-and-so and check on **this-n-that.**" (No incoming calls!)

• **GOOD LIGHTING** to illuminate every wall and all work areas. General overhead lighting is fine.

• Room to accommodate rolling **MEDIA CART** if video, music, or other media will be needed—they will! Music should be playing before the second person enters every day. (First to arrive selects opening music. Complaining about music is Blocking = $1. Be first tomorrow.)

• **BOOK SHELF** with dictionary; large single-volume, heavily illustrated encyclopedia; and other reference books (see "Creativity to Go" at the back of the book). This may be supplemented with additional books relevant to each project. (Here's where one Internet-enabled computer may be useful for quick, targeted searches ONLY. However, searches **can** be done LATER when they do not interrupt the creative flow, or during a break.)

• LARGE, serious **DO NOT DISTURB** sign outside the door.

• Air conditioning. Brainstorming is an activity for alert minds, so start with 68 degrees. (Warmer rooms slow thinking.) Stock up on "brainstorming blankets" (see "Brainstorming Is Cool" earlier in this chapter).

Love-to-Have Elements ... for Your Sandbox:

If you can create a permanent sandbox or three, here are the "Love-to-Have" elements for brainstorming **in addition** to the items on the previous pages:

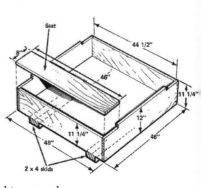

- **TRACK LIGHTING**: facing the walls, with dimmers. The table and work areas will be lighted by "spill" from track lights.
- Separate **TASK LIGHTING** directly lighting table and work areas, also on dimmers.
- Built-in **MEDIA CENTER** with Blue-ray/ DVD/CD player, iPod hook-up, and a medium-size, flat-screen TV. Cable TV hookup is good for big-news days.
- Collection of CDs with a wide variety of instrumental (no lyrics) music to set mood, spur thinking, relax, inspire, and celebrate before sessions and during breaks. **START A CD LIBRARY**: everyone suggest a favorite CD or two.
- Small "refridgamarator" with an ample supply of fruit juice, soft drinks, water, etc.
- **ALTERNATIVE SEATING** Bean bag chairs, sofa, hammock (in addition to swivel chairs).
- **Internet:** Wireless access is nice, though, for my money, the human mind is the most powerful, inventive tool during Creative Thinking and should be as free of distractions as possible. (If all you have are the memories and collective experiences of your seven team members, you will have at least three million ideas **to start with** on any given subject.)

Computers are distracting and will reduce human interaction. Think of it as "electronic side conversations." Not all brainstorming professionals agree with me on this point. (They can't be right about everything.) There will be ample time to surf the web between sessions. That said, in the right hands, ONE computer can get you to lots of web resources fast. But don't consider it a key element for creative thinking. It's best just to keep a running list of subjects to research **later**.

Similarly, I don't run and grab a dictionary (while creating lists of ideas) to be certain my lists, and index cards are spelled correctly. Fear not, in a group of seven, there will be a former spelling bee champ, or can be fixed later by the office spelling sheriff who will happily stay after work and fix them.

Recap

 # BUILDING YOUR OWN SANDBOX

- **Large Room**—Ample walking space, comfortable swivel chairs, large table (room for seven with elbow room for all). Enough space to break into smaller groups.
- **Cool Temperature**—If people comment (complain) that "it's too cold" that's good.
- **Wall Space**—Maximum pin-able surface (floor-to-ceiling) to present images, lists, doodles, magazine pages, ANY materials that may be used to stimulate thinking. Lots of room to post every idea. **Remember: Think, Say, Write** (post it on the wall!).
- **Art Supplies**—Small, cheap, felt pens (many colors) for note taking, doodling, storyboarding. **Large** ("jumbo") felt pens to list ideas on **large, sticky-note pads.**
- **Two easels**—Of the sturdy, FOUR-LEGGED variety. If you have to hold onto the easel while writing so it won't tip over, get rid of it. Donate to someone you don't like.
- **Media**—Built-in or portable cart: Blue-ray/DVD/CD player, iPod hookup, and good speakers.
- **Good lighting**—Everywhere (dimmers, if possible).
- **Food Table**—Ample supply of cool and hot drinks (all day) and snacks (fruit, baked goods ... poll the team), room to bring in lunch (a small fridge is great).
- **Mood**—Start the day with music. Play music during breaks. During all-day sessions I will take a five-minute music-only break every sixty to ninety minutes. This is not a break, but a time to reflect, think, and reread the walls and your notes.
- **WRAP-UP**—Decide when you will reconvene, homework assignment, and where are we going for dinner? (If the boss pays, keep creating over dinner.)

🕲 **TRY THIS**—The last five minutes of each session (whether it has been a few hours or a full day) play music without lyrics and encourage everyone to look around at all your ideas and make notes of any new ideas that occur to them. Spend a few minutes sharing ALL those new, inspired, yet unexpressed thoughts.

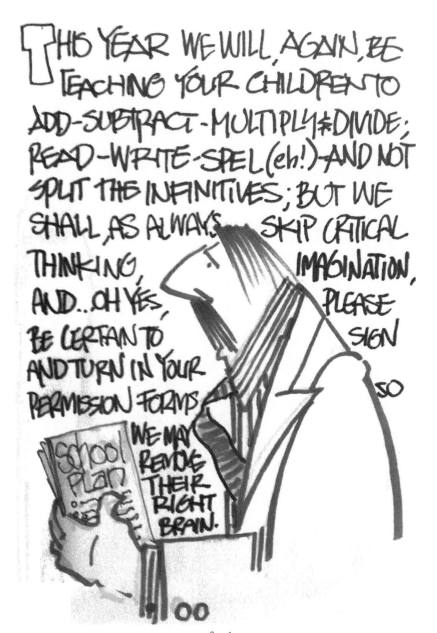

fig. 1
"Doodle's Demise": Day One.
Far too many studies indicate that the first day of school is the beginning of the end of our natural curiosity and our childhood propensity to express ourselves visually.

THE DOODLE FACTOR
[*visual note taking*]

This is the last chapter of this book ... that I wrote. The book was finished, edited (twice), complete, polished, and re-polished. It was perfect. The dictionary defines *perfect* as complete, thorough, finished.

Perfect
    adjective
    1. characteristics; as good as it is possible to be
    2. complete, absolute
    3. containing all necessary properties to accomplish and fulfill
       the task

Everything that needed to be in these pages was in. My *objective* for the book had been met. Chapter after chapter demonstrated how any organization, team, staff, or group can learn real brainstorming and use it to invent, create, design, or solve any challenge. Their primary tool for working together positively will be the **7 Agreements of Brainstorming**. My work here was done. Hah!

☞ Visual Thinking

That was a couple weeks ago—literally. Then, during a break in one of my half-day workshops in Toronto, a participant commented that he was initially quite resistant to my insistence that everyone take notes, *all day*, on blank (unlined) paper and *use the colored felt pens* that everyone had been given as they entered.

"I'm not an artist. I'm a matter-of-fact, logical person. But *today*, I am taking the best notes ever and loving it. What did you do to me, McNair?!"

He was excited, mystified, and inspired.

"You do have a creative spirit; today you kicked open the door leading to your more creative self. It's always been there, and now you know it."

"I sure do," he said.

"And there's no going back."

"Where do I get little pens like these? I want to get a bunch for my whole staff."

"One word—Target, Walmart, or a drugstore ... and get the cheap ones so you can buy lots of them."

fig. 2

Virtually all my note taking is in my sketchbooks. Above, notes from a recent conference I attended. Notice the use of BIG LETTERS, color (trust me), an arrow, boxes (a.k.a. "frames"), and a dialogue balloon: "Thank You!" All these simple doodles give my notes emphasis and priority and make them easy to review quickly for key ideas even months after doodling them. As for cartoons: The more you doodle people, the better they get and the more they enliven your notes. **The only "wrong way" to doodle is to NOT doodle.** This is NOT a test. [The second half of this chapter is a quick and easy doodle handbook: **McNair's Fearless Field Guide to Doodling**.]

I can only imagine what his staff must have thought when this already successful leader returned with the rest of his brain suddenly and newly energized.

This is not the only conversation I've had about the transformative power of *visual thinking*. At nearly every place I speak, consult, and teach, participants comment enthusiastically on how much they are enjoying and learning from my "forcing" them to take notes in color, *without* lines, and using simple images—*doodles*.

As often as not this leads to a conversation on all the captivating research available on the power of accessing our visual receptors while taking notes. Of the five senses, it is through *sight* that we take in 75 percent of what we know. We spend our early years pointing and asking, "What's that, mommy?"

When we take notes the *old-fashioned*, less effective way, we are creating page after page of lines of words. With a textbook we read, highlight, and take notes. And your notes look just like the pages of verbiage you are attempting to capture. What have you accomplished? Even if you use the authorized method of outlining: Roman numerals, numbers, and letters, there is little emphasis on anything. All words look the same—the same as each other and the same as the text you are studying. If you simply added BIG LETTERS, arrows, boxes, stars, and color, your retention of the information would expand tremendously.

You used to draw, every day!

We all did. What happened? When we were young—before we started school we drew everything, all the time. A big reason was we couldn't yet read or write. Yet we never stopped to reflect, *"What am I doing? I can't draw."* That didn't stop us because we didn't know there were rules. We didn't know, yet, that some people CAN draw and most of us CANNOT—or do not. But while we were drawing, scribbling, and doodling, we were learning. We were watching all of life around us. As we observed, we were learning with our eyes and recording it in the best way we could: with pictures, colors, and shapes. The sky was a thick band of blue across the top of the page we drew. Why? Because we looked up and there it was, *blue sky*, right above us.

The world was our classroom, construction paper our note pad, and a box of sixty-four crayons were our note–taking instruments. We saw better back then. We noticed colors and size, and the more we noticed, the more we learned. We learned because we "wrote it down" in *pictures*. Then, as now, **75 percent of what we learned came through what we saw.**

So if we are taking notes from what we see in a textbook and it is mostly or completely text, our notes will be mostly words. We may return later with a bright highlighter to add a bit of emphasis. But it is only a bit. Really the highlighter is an editing tool. We are saying THIS (bright line through a word or phrase) is the important information, and THIS is the key date, definition, or formula. You could write a couple of sentences to remind yourself that the **U.S. Constitution** was ratified in 1781. But what if, instead of words you doodled:

– an American flag

– a ☐ with writing inside (doodled **"U.S. Constitution"**)

– big, old-time numbers: **1781**

(Doodle above found in my editor's notes along with all his marks, was this full-sail proofreader's notation.)

Visual Note Taking

But what if we started with pictures and colors? What if our first notes on the text, lecture, or session were already highlighted because we used colored markers for every word we wrote? And what if some of our "notes" were pictures—simple, quickly drawn, scribbled (just for you). That's why I expect everyone in all my seminars and in-house corporate training and brainstorming sessions to grab a fist full of blank (unlined) paper and a few colored felt pens for ALL their note taking. I am not asking my seminar participants to be Rembrandt or da Vinci. I don't even expect you to draw as well as the simple saints found in Charlie Schulz's *Peanuts* gallery.

If a picture is worth a THOUSAND words, a DOODLE should count for a couple hundred at least.

"When you leave here, you are welcome to return to the world of every-stroke-is-the-same ballpoint pens and every-line-is-the-same-size note pads." But everything is NOT of the same importance. Visual note taking (including doodling) is a great way to give value to key parts of your notes. And it's fun to do. And more fun to re-read later than pages of words.

That's why I expect everyone to try it for the hour or four that they are with me.

"Not a chance," said one corporate VP not long ago. (His team made him try it.)

If your notes really are all the same, why bother trying to record even one word? But, if something the speaker says (or the textbook editors have written) sticks out, pokes us in any way, why not make notes that stick out? What would it be like to go over your notes later and have the visuals poke back at you?

Highlighters don't poke. They may turn up the volume a notch or two, but not enough. If your initial notes were written in the same quiet strokes of your rollerball, the highlighter cranks it up only to four or five.

In the "mockumentary" film *Spinal Tap*, filmmakers follow a fictitious heavy metal band of the same name. At one point lead guitarist, Nigel Tufnel (actor Christopher Guest), explains his band's success.

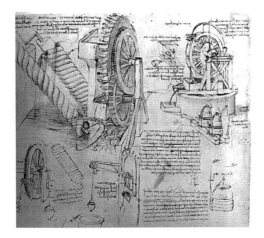

fig. 3
Leonardo da Vinci's studies for moving water uphill.
Notice there are more drawings than words.

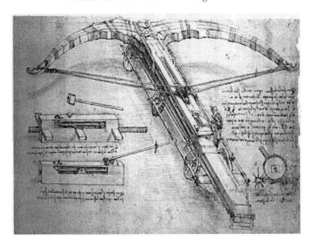

fig. 4
Leonardo's mechanical variations for the crossbow.
Again the details in his drawing make lengthy notes and explanation unnecessary.

"Most bands have guitar amplifiers with a volume control from one to ten. Look: Ours go to ELEVEN! Don't you see, *eleven* … it's louder than ten." (Find it on YouTube.)

Visual note taking is *eleven*, fifteen, or twenty-seven!

I am not asking you to make art. I want you to *doodle* and to doodle as well as *you* doodle. The doodle guide in this chapter will assist you in getting better at doodling and having more fun doodling it.

This is not a test.

Visual Thinking, Spatial Learning, or Right-Brain Learning

Doodling may actually help us absorb more information. In a study published in *Applied Cognitive Psychology* (Vol. 24, Issue 1), professor Jackie Andrade (University of Plymouth in Britain) played a rambling voice-mail message to forty people, half of whom were given shapes to fill in as they listened. The result was astonishing. The doodlers recalled 29 percent *more* of the message than those who just listened. Prof. Andrade says that apparently idle scribbling uses just enough cognitive bandwidth to stave off daydreaming, so doodling seems to actually help us focus. He also asserts that doodling is far more productive than merely daydreaming. And … doodling requires *less* brain work than daydreaming. (Professor Andrade's full article, "What Does Doodling Do?", is widely available online.)

The uber-techie magazine *Wired* reported in June 2009: "Good news, doodlers: What your colleagues consider a distracting, time-wasting habit (doodling) may actually give you a leg up on them by helping you pay better attention."

Love da Vinci's art. I'm adding doodles to my lab books!

Doodling—often called "visual thinking"—as a method of recording thoughts is not at all new.

Probably the best example of visual note taking, and my favorite, is Leonardo da Vinci (*previous page.*) He was simultaneously an artist, scientist, inventor, and cartographer.

The art world will say we cannot fully appreciate his art without looking at his science. Meanwhile, the scientific community says that da Vinci's science cannot be understood without examining his detailed art. Cracking Mr. da Vinci's code requires deciphering his doodles. Leonardo's techniques are most ably and engagingly explored in Michael Gelb's inspiring book *How to Think Like Leonardo da Vinci: Seven Steps to Genius Every Day.*

(It is, of course, heavily illustrated.) In his follow-up book, *Innovate Like Edison*, Gelb reproduces pages from Edison's notebooks. Many pages contain far more

[a.]

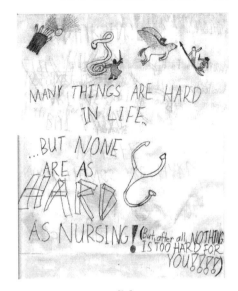

[b.]

[c.]

[d.]

fig. 5: a, b, c, and d

Four "full pages" of visual note taking: [b] class notes from my lawyer/author friend John, now in nursing school; [a and c] from McNair sketchbook pages at various conferences, [d.] When **Allison Crow** first sent this page I was excited because I could access her thoughts quickly using the visual cues she used to point to key information. (All pages used by permission.)

Right: Felt pen on paper towel sketched while writing this chapter and having my smoked chicken salad and glass of 2006 Bordeaux.

drawings than words. Both da Vinci and Edison knew the power of sketching their inventions to work out the task at hand, as well as communicating it to others. We are still building da Vinci's designs *today*.

The experts could have asked me in second grade, or earlier. I knew way back then that doodling helped me pay attention and aided my learning. My incessant doodling drove an endless parade of teachers crazy. Mses. Wiseman, Smallfoot (real name), Sarton, Douglas, Frances, and Fagin all took turns reprimanding me for "not paying attention in class" or turning in "sloppy," "messy" homework. This meant that no matter how well I had addressed the subject at hand with my thoughts (in word form) my doodles in the margins constituted bad work. I was always happy to point out how my art *illustrated* my homework.

Never mind that I got good grades, mostly. I hated algebra and loved geometry. Math + art = geometry! History and geography, for me, required pictures. *Our textbooks are full of pictures*, I pointed out a few too many times. I was f-f-f-frequently turned over to the principal. (From grades three to eight that meant a trip to my father's office.) He was very creative, though not artistic and was always fascinated by my doodles.

We are daily surrounded by practical applications of visual thinking: stock market graphs, engineering schematics, advanced mathematics, aeronautics, green-yellow-red signal lights, architecture plans, maps, GPS, and IKEA furniture assembly instructions (virtually wordless). All of us can recognize labels in a grocery store from farther away than we can possibly read their words. Our memory is a picture album, a museum of art and design. All of learning is about recognizing shapes, colors, textures, and spatial relationships. On the most basic level we are all actively watching and seeing during every moment and in every corner of our lives.

Have you ever heard of anyone who dreams in text? Our visual thinking is snap, crackle, and popping as we drive, fly, navigate, and play chess, and sports, it's strategizing during full-contact Scrabble. There is not a single modern video game that does not tout itself as having the most realistic (lifelike, vivid) images of any game on the market. Would great sound effects and stick figures be enough? Hardly. No one is rushing to Best Buy to grab that great new game: **Grand Theft Fonts.** (I'm tingling.)

Even the simple act of playing catch requires our visual thinking to be at its best.

Drawing in Class ... Staff Meetings, Conferences, and Church

I want you to doodle and to DOodle it as well as *you* doodle. It need not be difficult or frustrating. The clear evidence is that visual note taking *as a part of* any note taking will improve your focus, and you will retain more information than just recording words. AND ... doodling requires less brain power than the traditional word way of recording. The mounting evidence is that doodling increases your retention 30 to 90 percent. Your mind will recall images—doodles—more quickly and vividly than words and sentences.

Little kids, just learning to talk, are encouraged by parents to "use your words." Now that you've got that part down, it's time to go back to your pre-words self and *use your pictures!*

The Sooner You Start

Whether you rarely doodle or never doodle, the best way to improve your doodling is to draw anything. And the best way to start is to doodle everything. We are not abandoning words, just enhancing them.

One of the most inspiring, playful artists I call on regularly is Hugh MacLeod and his back-of-the-business-card art at www.GapingVoid.com. Hugh sends me a doodle almost every day to inspire me. (Actually it's his email newsletter and it's free for anybody, but I choose to believe Hugh is doodling for me.) Hugh's humor runs from the sacred to the salty. His art is *wild*. And his book *Ignore Everybody* will show you doodling made powerful and still endlessly playful.

In developing this chapter I tested my visual thinking and doodling ideas on Facebook and my blog "Tea With McNair." The response was better than I could have hoped for—and from a wide variety of people. Steve Björkman, my longtime friend recalled our sixth-grade teacher saying, "Quit drawing in class, Stevie, that'll never get you anywhere." She gave me exactly the same "encouragement." Steve is now one of the most successful doodlers and illustrators in the land. Besides in his own kids' books, his doodles grace the pages of many other authors, including three by Jeff Foxworthy. I asked Steve not to "doodle and drive." He dashed off the self-portrait at right.

Make time to consciously doodle daily. Start with the simple exercises in my **Fearless Field Guide for Doodling**—*a few pages away!* The more you do it, the easier it becomes and the more it will feel natural for you to use visual note taking

everywhere. Doodle more, get better at it, enjoy it more, do it more.

In the 1990s a new tool called "mind mapping" swept through corporate board rooms. It is still used widely as an outlining, problem-diagramming tool. Mind mapping employs the visual imagery of a subject or problem topic at the center (in a circle or box) with multiple lines radiating out from the center, often leading to other boxes or circles forming a sub-hub. It all resembles a spider's web or the root system of a large tree. My only concern with mind mapping is when it contains only words. Then it is merely a graphic note-taking tool on a radial design, illustrating the relationship of ideas. It's like diagramming a sentence, but in all directions. Many mind maps (the best I've seen) add images, doodles, cartoons, and even pictures cut from magazines and company publications to illustrate the words on the diagram. Those maps can be read more quickly and communicate more dynamically.

If you are already using mind mapping, let me encourage you to add *color*, BIG-LETTERED WORDS, and doodles (stars, boxes, faces, "stick" figures) to your "spiders with words on their legs." That, of course, is the point of this chapter, to understand the power of integrating images into our written communications.

Imagine getting a map from your auto club—and there are pictures of key buildings and other landmarks along the route. That's a map anyone could follow and enjoy the trip even more ...

"There it is: The little windmill, just like on the map!"

Are you ready to doodle?

Post Scriptum

A famous American Japanese painter taught drawing for many years at a local college. One night, as he was headed out the door to an evening class, his little daughter asked, "Daddy, where are you going?"

"I'm going to the college to teach my drawing class."

"But it's night time. Isn't it too late for kids to go to school?"

"I teach drawing to grown-ups, honey."

After letting this sink in for a moment she said, "Did they forget how?"

"People who never make mistakes, never make anything new."

Albert Einstein

This Just In ...

The word *doodle* dates back to early seventeenth century, meaning *fool* or *simpleton*, from German *dudel*, to play! (Originally used in the context of playing bagpipes or *dudel*.) In American English the word *dude* might actually be a derivation of *doodle*.

"Fool, simpleton" is the intended meaning in the song *Yankee Doodle*, first sung by British troops before the American Revolutionary War. In the early eighteenth century there was a verb *to doodle*, meaning "to swindle or to make a fool of." The modern word *doodle* burst upon the scene in the 1930s from "dawdle"—meaning wasting time, being lazy, or completing a task *slowly*.

In the classic film *Mr. Deeds Goes to Town*, Mr. Deeds mentions "doodle" as a "made up word" that describes scribbling. "It helps a person think," says Longfellow Deeds. Some film historians credit *Mr. Deeds'* screenwriter Robert Riskin as inventor of the word.

Even powerful Google has added doodled logos to their title pages.

Calling All Doodlers! Send *YOUR* doodles and visual note taking examples for possible inclusion in future editions of **HATCH!** (the book) and the online HATCH! Facebook page:

www.facebook.com/Hatch-by-McNair-Wilson

And now, *the pages you've all been waiting for.*

McNAIR's
FEARLESS
FIELD GUIDE
TO DOODLING
&
VISUAL THINKING
FOR EVERYONE

CMcNair

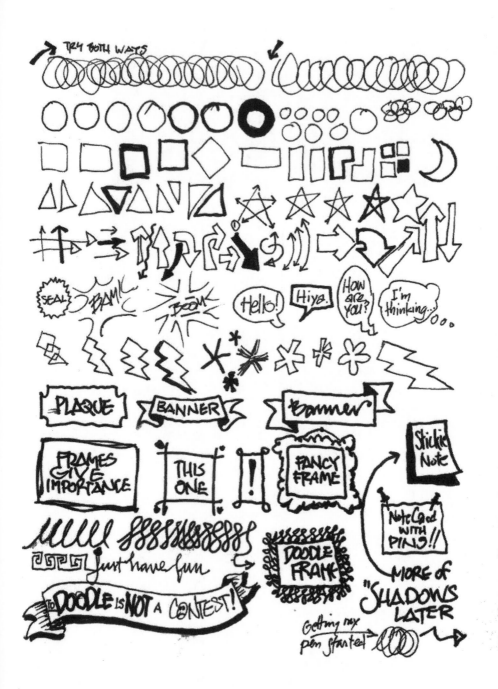

fig. 6
Instructions: 1. Doodle all of the above; 2. Repeat, f-f-f-frequently

:: TOOL KIT ::

YOU WILL NEED A FEW SIMPLE TOOLS ~ ALL AVAILABLE AT WALGREENS (ANY LARGE DRUG STORE) OR TARGET, WALMART, ETC.

- *SKETCHBOOK* (SEE PHOTO) A SIMPLE, SPIRAL-BOUND (8X10 OR 9X12 INCH) NO SMALLER (YOU WANT A BIG PAGE TO DOODLE FREELY), AND NO BIGGER (NOT SO LARGE THAT YOU WILL NOT WANT TO TAKE IT WITH YOU *EVERYWHERE*).

- *DOODLE PENS* (NOT BALLPOINT OR ANY OTHER WRITING INSTRUMENT YOU HAVE BEEN USING ON A REGULAR BASIS. FOR NOW, WE ARE

fig.7

Spiral sketchbook and a couple simple felt pens

TURNING A CORNER: TRYING SOMETHING NEW, LOOKING AT THE WORLD WITH NEW EYES. SO WE NEED NEW WAYS TO CAPTURE & RECORD WHAT WE SEE & HEAR. GRAB A FEW DIFFERENT STYLES AND BRANDS OF SMALL "FELT-TIP" OR FIBER-POINT PENS. GET DIFFERENT COLORS AND JUST PLAY ... COLORED PENCILS, OK. (INSTRUCTIONS BELOW.)

WARNING (AND A SUGGESTION) :: IF YOU ARE NOT NOW MUCH OF A DOODLER AND ARE NEW TO THE WORLD OF VISUAL THINKING, *DO NOT* START WITH AN EXPENSIVE, HARDCOVER SKETCHBOOK AND FANCY ART PENS. YOU WILL NOT FEEL FREE TO DOODLE, SCRIBBLE, AND PLAY WITH SUCH TOOLS. INEXPENSIVE TOOLS WILL FREE YOU TO PLAY: DOODLE, SCRIBBLE, AND MAKE A MESS ... ON *EVERY PAGE, EVERYDAY!*

THERE ARE LOTS OF WAYS TO DOODLE: DRAW, SCRIBBLE ... THIS *FIELD GUIDE* OFFERS A FEW SIMPLE PROMPTS TO JUMP-START THE HESITANT NOVICE & ENCOURAGE THOSE WHO ARE EAGER TO EXPAND THEIR RANGE OF CHOICES. WHEREVER YOU ARE ON THE DOODLE-ARCHY, THERE WILL BE IDEAS AND SIMPLE-TO-FOLLOW METHODS TO ASSIST YOU IN HAVING FUN AND THINKING OUT LOUD AND IN COLOR.

:: SHAPES: Sticks and circles and boxes ::

1. *START* BY WARMING UP YOUR PEN, WRIST, AND ARM BY DRAWING *SPIRALS* ACROSS THE PAGE, MAKING *CIRCLE* SHAPES. (USE UNLINED PAPER.) USING FLUID, CONSISTENT MOVEMENT IS THE GOAL (SEE OPPOSITE PAGE).
2. *NOW, MAKE SEPARATE CIRCLES . . .* THEN OTHER SHAPES:
    - SQUARES & RECTANGLES
    - TRIANGLES & STARS
    - ARROWS (STICK & BOXY)
    - SEALS, EXPLOSIONS, AND
    - LIGHTNING BOLTS, ASTERISKS ...
- THE ABOVE LIST (AND EXAMPLES, PREVIOUS PAGE) ARE THE MOST COMMON DOODLES DRAWN WHILE TALKING ON THE PHONE, IN MEETINGS,

ABCDEFGHIJKL

MNOPQRSTUV

WXYZ 1 2 3 4 5 6

a a a a a a   b b b b b
1. 2. 3. 4. 5.   1. 2. 3. 4. 5.

TRY THIS! → MAKE BIG

FAT LETTERS

JUST ONE WORD MAKES A BIG Difference on a page of NOTES

AABBCCDEEFGGHHII
JJKLLMMNNO-PPQQ
RRSSTTUUVVWWXXYYZZ

Those little marks are called "SERIFS"

A "SERIF"   A "san Serif"

Try Printing You Alphabet and add SERIFS

[INK SMUDGES of AUTHENTICITY]

OR CLASS. NO ONE THINKS OF IT AS ART. (IF YOU ARE NEW TO DOODLING OR HAVEN'T DOODLED "ON PURPOSE" SINCE CHILDHOOD, IT'S WORTH FILLING AN ENTIRE PAGE WITH EACH GROUP OF SHAPES FROM THE LIST ABOVE. EVERYTHING ELSE BUILDS ON THOSE BASIC SHAPES.)

"DIALOGUE BALLOONS"

ALPHABETS

3. ALPHABETS: SIMPLE PRINTING, BIG WORDS, BLOCK LETTERS (EXAMPLES AT LEFT)

1. PRINT YOUR ABC'S IN BOTH UPPER AND LOWERCASE (INCH HIGH OR BIGGER).
2. REPEAT, BUT THIS TIME MAKE EACH LETTER THICKER BY WRITING OVER IT TWO OR THREE TIMES. THE IDEA IS TO MAKE EACH LETTER BOLDER BUT STILL READABLE.
3. NOW MAKE THICKER LETTERS BY OUTLINING THEM TO FORM BOX LETTERS.
4. TRY FORMING BOX LETTERS AROUND SINGLE-STROKE LETTERS AS I HAVE DONE WITH THE NUMBERS 1 TO 6 ON OPPOSITE PAGE.
5. TRY MAKING BOX LETTERS WITHOUT FIRST DRAWING THE SINGLE STROKE. HAVE FUN. THE ONLY "RULE" IS READABILITY.
6. NOTICE HOW THE BASIC SHAPES (CIRCLE, SQUARE, RECTANGLE), ARE USED IN EACH LETTER.

***LETTERING RULE NO. 1 : "CLARITY OVER CLEVERNESS"
– NO MATTER WHAT, IT HAS TO BE READABLE***

- I HAVE BEEN "PLAYING" WITH LETTERING ALL MY LIFE. THE TITLE OF THIS BOOK (BELOW) WAS DOODLED ON A PAPER TOWEL ~ GIVING THESE LETTERS GREAT TEXTURE!

• IN 1992 I DIRECTED A STAGE PRODUCTION OF *CYRANO DE BERGERAC.*
I DOODLED "CYRANO" OVER AND OVER TO DEVELOP THE FINAL LOGO
(BOTTOM) WE USED FOR POSTERS, ETC. BELOW IS A TINY SAMPLE OF
THE SORT OF "GOOFING AROUND" I WOULD HAVE DONE TO CONCOCT
MY FINAL HAND-LETTERED LOGO. VARYING WIDTHS ARE DONE WITH
FELT PENS THAT HAVE A "BRUSH TIP" LIKE A PAINT BRUSH. (CHECK YOUR
LOCAL ARTIST SUPPLY STORE. THESE PENS HAVE A MIND OF THEIR
OWN AND WILL GIVE YOU "HAPPY ACCIDENTS" IN LETTERING AND OTHER
DOODLES.)

MAKE A FACE

4. MAKE A FUNNY FACE . . . ON PAPER: WE'LL START WITH BASIC SHAPES FROM THE FIRST EXERCISE.
- DRAW A FEW SQUARES & CIRCLES (IN THE SPACE BELOW)
- ADD A FACE: A FEW DOTS AND A LINE FOR MOUTH, LIPS, EYES, HAIR . . . ;•)

DRAW HERE. . .

- IF YOU CAN DRAW THE FIRST FACE (BELOW LEFT), CAN YOU ADD A BIT AND DRAW THE SECOND ... THE THIRD, FOURTH ... ?
- **CHANGE THE SHAPE** OF THE HEAD: OVAL, SQUARE, OR ... AND MAKE A FACE IN EACH.

IN YOUR "SPARE-TIME DOODLING" START ADDING FACES ~
MOVE BEYOND SHAPES AND FILLING IN "O" IN "HOTEL" & "MOTEL"

MORE FACES

- **LOOK AT A FRIEND'S FACE**, OR FACES IN A MAGAZINE OR **YOUR FACE IN A MIRROR**. WHAT DO YOU SEE? WHAT ARE A FEW KEY LINES THAT COULD MAKE YOUR FACE DOODLES MORE THAN DOTS AND LINES IN A CIRCLE? A LINE UNDER THE MOUTH TO SHOW THE LOWER LIP, A VERTICAL LINE FOR THE BRIDGE OF THE NOSE, SHAPE OF EYES BY ADDING THE EYELID OR EYELASHES ...

- **ADD EARS, HAIR**, MUSTACHE ,,, OR BEARD ... NECK, NECKLACE, EARRINGS, SHIRT COLLAR & TIE, HAIR RIBBON, HAT, LIPSTICK ...

BALLOON HEAD

(SEE EXAMPLE BELOW)
IN THE SPACE BELOW, DRAW BALLOON HEADS: UPSIDE DOWN, SIDEWAYS, RIGHT-SIDE-UP ... THEN ADD FEATURES ... THE MORE YOU DOODLE, THE LESS YOU WILL CARE ABOUT THE OUTCOME AND THE BETTER YOU WILL DOODLE.

- *NO. 1 STARTS WITH A BALLOON SHAPE* THEN HAIR, MUSTACHE, NOSE, GLASSES, AND BODY ARE ADDED. AT LEFT, TRY MAKING A FEW BALLOON HEADS. VARY THE SIZE AND SHAPE OF THE BALLOONS.

NO. 1 ~ BUILDING A BALLOON HEAD   NO. 2 ~ BALLOON HEAD

- *NO. 3 STARTS WITH A BALLOON* TURNED UPSIDE DOWN. BY ADDING A FEW SIMPLE FEATURES, IT BECOMES. . .

GEORGE WASHINGTON
AS SEEN ON THE ONE DOLLAR
BILL

STICK FIGURES AND BEYOND

INSTRUCTIONS: BEGIN ON TOP ROW WITH THE FIGURE YOU CAN DRAW, MOVE RIGHT ADDING DIMENSION AND DETAIL. CREATE YOUR OWN PEOPLE: COWBOY, ATHLETE, CHEF, MAD HATTER ...STICK FIGURES ... AND THEIR FATTER FRIENDS

- STICK FIGURES ARE LIKE THE THE SINGLE-STROKE ALPHABETS WE STARTED WITH A FEW PAGES AGO. IF YOU EVER PLAYED "HANGMAN" ON THE BUS TO CAMP, YOU CAN DRAW STICK FIGURES.
- JUST LIKE WITH OUR SINGLE-STROKE ALPHABETS, WE NEXT ADD A FEW LINES TO MAKE OUR STICK PEOPLE THICKER—TRY VARYING LINES ON LEGS, ARMS, ETC.
- IF YOU DRAW AROUND THE FATTENED FIGURES (LIKE WITH BOX LETTERS) YOU CAN DRAW PEOPLE THAT ARE MORE FILLED-OUT—AS IN THE FIGURES ON THE MIDDLE LINE ON THE OPPOSITE PAGE. *YOUR TURN* :
  1. *MAKE A FEW SIMPLE STICK PEOPLE.*
  2. *ADD A FEW STROKES TO EACH LINE* TO MAKE YOUR PEOPLE THICKER.
  3. *TRANSFORM* YOUR LEAN LONG-DISTANCE RUNNERS INTO FILLED-OUT *REGULAR FOLKS*.
  4. JUST AS WE USED DIFFERENT SHAPES (CIRCLES, BOXES, BALLOONS) START WITH A SHAPE AS THE TORSO AND ADD ARMS, LEGS, HANDS, AND EXPRESSIVE FACES.

ABOVE::
SIMPLE CIRCLE HEAD WAS A SMALL DOODLE ON A FULL PAGE OF NOTES IN ONE OF MY SKETCHBOOKS. THE SPEAKER MENTIONED A SURVEY THAT INDICATED THAT 58 PERCENT OF PEOPLE NEVER READ ANOTHER BOOK ~ *NOT ONE* ~ AFTER GETTING OUT OF *HIGH SCHOOL*. (EVEN IN COLLEGE MANY STUDENTS READ "CLIFFS NOTES" OR ONLINE SUMMARIES.)
   CONGRATULATIONS FOR NOT BEING IN THAT 58 PERCENT AND FOR READING AT LEAST ONE MORE BOOK - THIS ONE!

DOODLE ANYTHING YOU SEE. DOODLE *EVERYTHING*. DOODLE OFTEN.
30 MIN. A DAY WILL MAKE DRAMATIC IMPROVEMENT IN JUST A FEW WEEKS.

OTHER TRICKS

DON'T BE STOPPED BY THAT LITTLE VOICE IN YOUR HEAD THAT SAYS, *"I CAN'T DRAW!"* IF IT'S *INSIDE* YOU, IT IS *SMALLER* THAN YOU. YOU CAN OVERPOWER IT ~ *SHOVE A FELT PEN UP ITS NOSE! DO IT NOW!*

THE OTHER OBSTACLE TO ADDING CARTOON PEOPLE AND FUN ALPHABETS TO YOUR DOODLING MAY COME FROM LOOKING AT MY DOODLES IN THESE PAGES. "I COULD NEVER DO THAT." WELL, IF YOU NEVER TRY IT, *YOU'RE RIGHT*. BUT, I'VE BEEN DOODLING ON *PURPOSE* SINCE I WAS THREE YEARS OLD, IN CHURCH. I HAVE MORE THAN ONE HUNDRED FORTY SKETCHBOOKS FILLED WITH MY DOODLES. MOST ARE *NOTHIN'*.

THE FEW GOOD THINGS THROUGHOUT THIS BOOK ARE SOME OF THE BETTER DRAWINGS FROM MY DECADES OF DOODLES. WHATEVER *YOU DO BEST* IS LIKELY BECAUSE YOU HAVE DONE IT *A LOT*—OVER AND OVER AND OVER AND OVER AND ... WHETHER IT'S A SPORT, AN ARTISTIC ABILITY, OR CARD TRICKS, PRACTICE MAKES PERFECT. (THIS CHAPTER BEGAN WITH THE DEFINITION OF *"PERFECT"*: COMPLETE, THOROUGH, FINISHED ... "AS GOOD AS IT IS POSSIBLE TO BE." *YOU ARE ALREADY PERFECT* AT MORE THAN ONE SKILL. YOU WEREN'T BORN ABLE TO DRIVE A CAR—DID YOU GET OVER THAT?

ANYTHING CAN BE IMPROVED UPON. MY OWN DOODLES HAVE IMPROVED IN THE WEEK THAT I HAVE SPENT ADDING THIS CHAPTER TO *HATCH*. IT HAS ENCOURAGED ME TO DOODLE EVEN MORE THAN I DO NOW—WHICH IS ALMOST DAILY.

GRAB A SPIRAL SKETCHBOOK (TODAY) AND FILL IT AS FAST AS YOU CAN WITH THE EXERCISES IN THIS BOOK. (HAVE A LOOK, TOO, AT THE OTHER "VISUAL THINKING" RESOURCES I RECOMMEND AT THE END OF THIS CHAPTER & THE BACK OF THE BOOK.)

NO. 7. MEANWHILE, HERE ARE A FEW ADDITIONAL SHAPES AND TRICKS TO ADD TO YOUR NOTE TAKING IN CONFERENCES, MEETINGS, SCHOOL, BIBLE STUDY, ETC.

TRY FILLING SEVERAL PAGES OF YOUR NEW SPIRAL SKETCHBOOK WITH THE IMAGES AND TECHNIQUES ON THE OPPOSITE PAGE. HAVE FUN DOODLING ::

- HANDS, HEADS, & FACES
- ARROWS & POINTING HANDS
- BOXES, SPHERES, DIALOGUE BALLOONS
- GLOBES & MAPS
- LIGHT BULBS, WOOD GRAIN, LEAF, CAR, BOOK, BIRTHDAY CAKE, SOLAR SYSTEM ...

ANY OBJECT CAN BE MADE TO JUMP OFF THE PAGE WITH A "DROP SHADOW," 3D EFFECT. DRAW ANY SHAPE (LIKE THE BIG PLUS SIGNS, RIGHT) AND ADD 3D BY SIMPLY ADDING A DARKER COLOR TO THE *LEFT* OR *RIGHT* SIDE AND ALSO THE *TOP* OR *BOTTOM*.

LEFT/TOP   RIGHT/TOP   L/BOTTOM   R./BOTTOM

Further Reading & Doodling Resources

The books most often sited on *visual thinking* include:
- **Visual Thinking,** Rudolf Arnheim (1969)
- **Experiences in Visual Thinking,** Robert McKim (1971)
- **Drawing on the Right Side of the Brain,** Betty Edwards (1979). This is the No. 1 book I recommend to everyone (especially families) for learning to expand and improve your ability to put on paper what you see— and have fun learning. Whether or not you have any interest in being an artist, the ability to render a thought in visual form is an invaluable tool (second only to public speaking). Betty Edwards' book teaches you to *see better* through fun, easy-to-do exercises. I go back to it often! *Try it.*

You will learn freedom to just doodle from Hugh MacLeod's *Ignore Everybody.* [Hilarious and a bit raw.]

More recently there is *In The Mind's Eye,* Thomas G. West's

ABOVE: FROM MY DOODLED NOTES "AT THE TATE MUSEUM, LONDON" (2005)

absorbing look at some of the great non-verbal minds of the twentieth century: Einstein, Edison, Churchill, and Tesla.

There's also the work of Dan Roam in his two playfully motivating books **The Back of the Napkin** and **Unfolding the Napkin** (*The Hands-On Method for Solving Complex Problems with Simple Pictures*).

WARNING: Dan Roam uses stick figures.

A grand example of the power of playful doodles is also in my favorite book on creativity in corporate life: **Orbiting the Giant Hairball** by **Gordon MacKenzie** (former creative guru at Hallmark). His book is a delight-full, doodle-filled, scribbles-in-the-margins, book of stories and solutions for getting more creativity into the workplace and thereby enjoying corporate life more—while being more productive.

Doodling Books

- Two books: **Doodle Diary: Art Journaling for Girls** and **Doodle Sketchbook: Art Journaling for Boys,** both by my friend Dawn DeVries Sokel, are both fun and easy books to encourage young people to continue what we all did naturally as children—*doodle*. I find them inspiring for people of any age.

- **The Creative License** by Danny Gregory is a very inspiring and encouraging work filled with good prompts and "permission to be an artist."
- While killing time in a big airport I saw—at the back of a book shop—a book with a solid black cover (*that'll never sell*) and hand printed title, **Steal Like An Artist**. Austin Kleon has drained most of the mystique out of being creative. (That's the stuff that stops us from trying to be more actively creative.) This is a fun to read (and look at) little book, packed with inspiring treasures. GRAB IT.
- **More books** on creativity are listed at the back of this book. Be certain to include a few of the *sixteen* books by author/artist/grand encourager **SARK** (one word, no periods, all caps). Start with *Juicy Pens, Thirsty Paper* on writing.

Yogi Berra
Philosopher, baseball catcher

ASSUME THIS
[after words]

You are surrounded by idiots! More and more it seems as though everyone you work with is a knuckle-dragging, mouth-breather whose family album is filled with crude cave drawings.

In a workshop not so long ago, I asked a room full of middle and upper management folks, "If you could change one thing about your work place, what would it be?"

A smartly dressed woman near the front, complained that she loved her career, but had worked for three different companies in seven years—all run by "incompetents." She bemoaned her current job and feared her next would again involve toiling under someone less capable.

"Count on it!" I said. "I guarantee that your next boss will be the biggest dunderhead yet."

Stunned, she asked, "How can you say that?"

Opening the conversation to the two hundred folks in the workshop, I asked, "How do I know this?"

Silence. Contemplation. Furrowed foreheads. "What is common to *every* job she's had?"

From the back: "The people are incompetent."

"*Yes, and* ..."

"The boss is dumb."

"*Yes, and* ...," I nudged. "What is the one constant in every company she's worked for?"

"She didn't research the company effectively in advance."

"You're thinking too hard," I said. "It's not a trick question. Every place she works there is ...? *Watch closely*." I said like a magician about to reveal the trick. "The common factor with every place she's worked was that ... (pointing dramatically)... *she* was there. Now, eighty-six jobs later, she's primed to expect her next boss, and the next, and the next, will also be dolts. So, they *will* be world-class knuckleheads! Why? Because that's what she *expects*, that's what she's *looking* for, and that's what she'll *see*. And that is all she'll see!"

Heads nodded, and I heard sighs of understanding. Some even jotted a note in their conference notebook.

"We see whatever we are looking for and what we want to see."

⑨ **DoYouSeeWhatISee?** Not one of us is perfect. One winter, at a weekend retreat on "Recapturing Your Family's Creative Spirit" with two hundred enthusiastic folks, all church-going families, a father approached me during dinner. He and his seven-year-old daughter had spent a slice of their afternoon on the ice rink. After several frustrating attempts at skating, the little girl declared with an exhausted harumph, "Daddy, I keep falling down!" :: "That's not how I see you." Helping her back onto her skates, for the seventh time, he said. "I see you as someone who keeps getting back up." Great dad. :: **We see what we look for.**

The woman with too many terrible bosses might have actually had a boss or two who was given a position that was beyond their abilities. But somewhere along her professional path, she developed a bias for bad bosses. The first one might actually have been incompetent. By the time I caught up with her, though, she had found regular solace and affirmation in identifying the ineptitude of every boss.

A parent or teacher on the lookout for kids misbehaving will not be disappointed. Kids do misbehave. "Kid" comes from the Greek for "loud and messy." What if, on the other paw, you were to spend a day trying to catch children being wonderful? Chances are, that is precisely what you would see—all day long.

Two Words to Change Your World

Here at Lunar Donut Labs we have discovered two words that, when placed side by side, can radically alter your life and the lives of everyone around you. Even if you're the only person in your life reading this book, it will still work. Here are two words that can dramatically alter the expectations you have of others: friends, coworkers, family, even strangers. Link these two words. Burn them into your frontal lobes as if they were *one* word. Use them in any new setting. Use them as a filter when meeting a job applicant, new coworker or even a new boss.

The first word hardly ever works without the second, but together they refocus vision, realign expectations, repurpose relationships, and fortify people to take on human obstacles. Just two words:

☞ Assume Brilliance®

That's it. Write it one hundred times on the chalkboard of your mind—oops, I mean large Post-it® flip chart. **Stamp** it on every page of the Operations Manual of your life. *Hatch* a plan to make it your *standard operating procedure* … with family, friends, coworkers, and strangers.

Look for and expect *brilliance* in everyone. Expect them to succeed radiantly at being themselves. They may or may not be as fabulous as you. That's not the point. "Being you" is *your* job. Anyone else will be as lousy at being you as you would at being them. What counts is whether you notice them being terrifically *themselves*.

For several years, I was artistic director of the highly acclaimed improvisational SAK Theatre company. On my weekly walkabouts, watching our street actors at EPCOT Center, I would offer two or three specific, *positive* observations about the performance of each "Saktor." Then a challenge: "How will your next show be *better?*"

I knew they were brilliant. That's why we hired them. They weren't always confident of that about themselves. But I expected to catch them in the act of being remarkable. Mostly I did, and I pointed it out to them. That bolstered them to reach for the next level of excellence in their performance.

Everyone enjoys a compliment. More importantly, we all need them. Just like hugs, or a hot, bracing shower, affirmation is good for us. Finding and pursuing our "soul purpose" in life is why we've been put here. Any affirmation encourages our forward progress. Each one of us—doing our best—can and will inspire others. That's what's behind the **7 Agreements of Brainstorming**: doing our best, as a team, and having fun doing it. The fun is the interplay (*Yes, and ...*) that leads to better and best.

Just in case this really is the only lifetime you get, why not reset your expectation meter to "brilliance."

It's not always easy to find that spark in others, but it will be great fun looking. And it is joyous when you, at last, discover it.

In all my travels it is always a challenge for me to uncover brilliance as I deal with the "counter people." Airline, rental car, and hotel employees all suddenly are in charge of my life because they have a name tag, a counter, and something they know I need. With each counter encounter, I try to find even a *little bit* of brilliance there. Mostly I find it. Too often I do not. But if I expected incompetence, I would see only that—and traveling would become unbearable. I always make an attempt to point out their brilliance, thank them for it, and have often tracked down a manager or supervisor to report "outrageously brilliant service by (*employee's name*)."

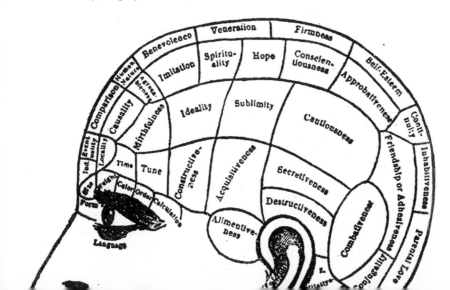

Leaving the jurisdiction of those in whom faint brilliance was detected, I sing to myself a favorite tune from Gilbert and Sullivan's magical operetta *The Mikado*. In it Koko, the Lord High Executioner, shares his inner-most thoughts. He's been keeping a secret list of candidates for the executioner's block, just in case they might one day run short of persons who need executing. He sings:

If someday it may happen that a victim must be found,
I've got a little list. I've got a little list.
Of society offenders who might well be underground,
And never would be missed.
No, they never would be missed!

He keeps a carefully prepared list of those in whom no brilliance has, thus far, been observed. Look again, dear Koko. Look long and look hard. Tear up your silly little list, your silly little list. And so should we all.

To **Assume Brilliance** means we do not maintain a mental scoreboard that keeps track of exactly how many times this person or that screwed up. Even if you should catch them being wonderful next Tuesday, you can say, "Ah ha! You may have shown a faint sign of terrific-ness here today, but, according to my records, on March 27, 1998, you really blew it. Remember? I certainly do. (Open small, black record book.) I have it right here. So today does not count."

We all need to stop keeping score and determine to keep on the lookout for each other's brilliance.

In the world of Assume Brilliance, no day counts but *right now*.

See brilliance? "Ah, ha! Now that's brilliant!" Worse case? You might scare someone who hasn't been paid a compliment or been recognized for their valuable contribution in quite some time.

Assume Brilliance in coworkers, bosses, subordinates, your spouse, kids, neighbor kids, and their goofball parents. With everyone you come in contact with, *Assume Brilliance*. Try it for a week and see what you see, and how people react when you point out their brilliance. The only thing that will change is your entire world.

A Story for All Parents

From third through eighth grades I attended a school where my father was the principal. I was sent to his office more than a few times every year for "cutting up," not focusing "on the work at hand," and other educational high crimes and misdemeanors. (This was long before ADD had been invented, so I was an unmedicated, highly distracted, gifted, hyperactive, bad speller. I always felt like "gifted" was the human version of a jelly donut. (I don't like jelly donuts.) *I just wanted to be a plain old chocolate donut ... no frosting.*)

A teacher complaining about me once told my parents, "He's the class clown!"

"Oh," said my dad, "I think you underestimate him. 'Class Clown' is so limiting. I suspect he is the Class *Circus*." (He told me about this years later.)

Today I'd be identified as a child with "alternative learning styles." (Jelly donut with sprinkles)

While I was at Walt Disney Imagineering, we hosted a two-day open house in the secretive inner sanctums of Walt's "dream factory." It was open to Imagineering employees and their immediate family members—ONLY. I got special dispensation for my parents to attend. There, just outside the front door of 1401 Flower Street, Glendale, California, I introduced my mom and dad to my boss, Marty Sklar (chairman of Disney Imagineering).

Talking about me becoming a theme park thinker-upper (Disney Imagineer) my dad told Marty, "We always knew his different way of approaching life would turn into something valuable someday."

"Thanks," Marty said, "for letting him be who he really is."

That was one of my best days at Disney—or anywhere on planet earth.

My parents assumed brilliance in my brother and me from the beginning and it paid off.

Moms and dads, take heed. Your kid ain't weird. Let her live what she loves. You won't be sorry when she becomes the conductor of the Chicago Symphony Orchestra. If you don't allow your son to paint, or dance, or read every book there is on chaos theory, someday he may leave and never call home (from his office on Mars). We need our creative weirdos to prevent the entire world from becoming one giant, color-controlled community of over-regulated beige boxes of stucco, and managed care in which all the music sounds the same (on and off of the elevator) and some federal agency tells us what we may and may not eat.

Don't just *allow* your children to do what they love, encourage them to pursue their passions and chase their dreams. Passion is not always as obvious as hair color, say, but can often be detected quite early. A good clue: When left alone to do whatever she wants to do, what sorts of activities will your daughter most often choose to fill her time?

Don't merely *allow* them to pursue their passions and dreams, be their cheerleader and biggest fan. Don't just *attend* their games and performances, jump in! When I taught high school theatre it rarely surprised me which parents would show up to volunteer with sets, costumes, and whatever needed getting done.

They were almost always the moms and dads of the best students. (Not the smartest, not even "A" students, just the best humans in a teenage body.)

One of the busiest friends I have is an author and speaker who travels all the time. Even so, he is also the coach of his son's soccer team. My friend Jim has consulted with world leaders, but he is never more delighted than when he is talking about Luke's soccer game. Paint and dance *with* your kids. Ask your young Einstein to "splain" chaos theory to you—it will be worth staying up late for. Time in your kid's life is an investment that ALWAYS pays off—now and for decades to come.

If you don't know what your kid loves, find out, and love it with them! When they come down for breakfast, be sitting at the kitchen table playing with clay. Be sure everyone in the family is late for school and work that day. Give them a note to take to the office. "Please excuse Albert's tardiness; it's Sculpture Day!" (Be sure the note is clay—or paint—stained.)

In all my seminars, corporate training, and private coaching I say to all parents of children of ANY age:

"Your unfulfilled dreams are NOT your children's To-Do list."

If you have a pulse tomorrow, get out *your* "To Dream" list and get dreaming. Few things will inspire your children as much as seeing you follow *your* passions.

It's time to make the donuts and fuel your rocket—there's a full moon tonight. Before the rooster crows at sunrise, you need to HATCH a plan. Maybe, for breakfast, instead of French toast … finger painting. Or finger painting with chocolate syrup. (Better stop by the store on the way home and get some.)

More Abundantly

In the most poetic of the four Gospels, John remembers Jesus calling himself the "son of man"—a servant of others. In John chapter ten, verse ten, Jesus says, "I have come that you might have *life* and that you might have it—"

How does this finish?

Abundantly.

Close, but no unleavened bread. John records Jesus as saying, "'I have come that you might have life, and that you might have it **more** abundantly!"

For Jesus mere abundance is not enough. He wants us to have life *more* abundantly! A more modern rendering of the New Testament says, "That you might have life *to the full*." Eugene Peterson's popular adaptation of the Bible—*The Message*—sets Jesus' words as, "More and better life than they ever dreamed of."

More abundantly! "More"… now where have we seen that word recently? The assumption of our Creator is that we are already *in* abundance—living rich, full, remarkable lives—and Jesus shows up with *more*—a fresh supply.

One day your door bell rings, and there's a guy with a brown cap, brown jacket, brown truck, and two big boxes, saying, "Here's your monthly shipment of abundance. Sign line seventeen."

All the while, there's a big aluminum shed in your backyard marked "Scarcity."
That shed is filled with boxes of file folders marked: *No Time; To Be Completed* ...;
*Never Got Around To; What Will People Say; Lost Interest; Not Enough Money; Awaiting
More Specific Instructions; Gave Up On;* and *Future Failures.* Yet here on your doorstep has
arrived *more* abundance—two big boxes.

Our Creator is saying, "Live all the life you want, there's plenty, and *here's more!*"
The only question now is, *How great can you stand it?* Live *more* abundantly. And don't
worry—you won't run out.

Creativity—it's not just for children, artists, theme park designers, NASA scientists,
teachers, camp directors, and donut makers anymore!

Assume that a piece of the Original Spark still burns within *you* and *everyone* with
whom you come in contact. Discovering that spark is the first light along the path to
finding your personal passion—your built-in reason for being. Find your passion, know
your purpose, live with power—and brilliance.

Use the best parts of you (brilliance) to interact and invent with coworkers, family
members, and friends. Creative thinking teams are about discovering (or rediscovering!)
our brilliance and putting it into action.

{*Pick three. Do one, daily. Repeat daily. Start now.*}
Understand this: The rest of us need you to do this—show your Brilliance. *I* need you
to do it.

That's why I look for the brilliance in everyone.

Imagine you, at your best, and a handful of your coworkers, all working together,
brilliantly and playfully and enjoying it. That does not need to be merely your imagination.
You can make it happen.

"If you don't do you, You doesn't get done and the world is incomplete... But when you do you, you inspire the world."

McNair

:: Illustration of me by Steve Björkman, artist, illustrator, greeting card mogul, and good friend and fellow doodler since sixth grade! ::

◄CKNOWLEDGMENTS

This started out as the little book of big ideas with doodles and a list of possible titles in a sketchbook … long, long ago. In my creativity seminars—from Modesto to Madrid, Spain—people asked, "Do you have all this in a book?" Taking what I do live at conventions and as in-house consulting and re-crafting it into a finished book is the result, in no small part, to the support, assistance, and encouragement of many people … most of them friends.

Michelle Capriario jump-started the writing process by transcribing recordings from my seminars.

Meanwhile, I created a storyboard to outline the book. I reread, rewrote, added and subtracted a lot from the transcript. That formed the first eight chapters.

Susan Kennedy (a.k.a. SARK, author-artist-speaker) longtime friend, proclaimed the first draft "a full-fledged book." (More on Susan … in a bit).

More friends read it—including several who had never seen the live, workshop version. Questions developed: *Explain the role of the facilitator. What if your budget is smaller than your wild ideas? What is storyboarding?*

All these great questions motivated the second act: practical tips on the where, who, and how of *brainstorming.*

Nina Diamond, who edited my book *Raised in Captivity*, edited an early draft of HATCH!

Illustrations were wedged in as I wanted it to feel like one of my sketchbooks. Mostly I used existing sketches—and new *stuff*—all from my own sketchbooks.

Wes & Judy Roberts encouraged and coached all along the way—for this book and for life in general … and life in *specific.*

Steve & Elaine Musick's hospitality of home and heart—and business wisdom.

Jeff van Kooten, professional cheerleader said, "I could use this now." Here 'tis, Kooter!

Jim Harvey (RIP), "It's about *time*, McNair!"

Bill Muir pushed me to make it all "more McNair."

Al Lunsford, mentor, friend, sage, and grand encourager. Al had a writer on his team who he sent to Oakland, California, to work on the entire manuscript:

Jim Hancock (also a longtime friend) and gifted author/wordsmith, spent a week in my loft holding my feet to the refiner's fire and my fingers to the Mac. Al Lunsford was our patron who made this week of open-manuscript surgery possible—and invited us for a "Fog City" lunch and progress report. Al asked, "Is it a different book?" It was indeed. Thanks, Al!

Jerry "B." Jenkins—longtime friend, mentor-cheerleader, movie-going pal. Jerry provided invaluable editorial insights and connected me with literary agent and friend:

Mark O. Sweeney presented my fully illustrated, spiral-bound manuscripts to a parade of publishers of business books on both coasts. A handful of editors were enthusiastic, but could not convince their marketing and sales geniuses to embrace it. ("We already have a book like that." Of course they don't.) After the rejections of eighteen publishers I was more anxious than ever to have actual books available for all the requests. Being rejected puts me in good company. I felt famous. [1.] Mark Sweeney was the first to advise me to publish it ASAP.

Andy Scheer—editor—came onboard at the eleventh hour with his wit and fine-toothed-editing comb in hand. Andy is also a longtime friend and so he gets my humor and conversational voice in print.

Favorite Eateries that let me camp out for hours with my sketchbook and MacBook to dream, write, doodle, and use their AC. In the East Bay, N. California: Rockridge Cafe, Montclair Egg Shop, César, Nikki's 24-Hour Cafe, Ole's Waffle Shop, and many afternoons at Rudy's Can't Fail Cafe (across from Pixar Studios, Emeryville, CA). I used up acres of butcher paper table coverings at Alice Waters' Chez Panisse in Berkeley.

Across the Bay in San Francisco: A16, *"the house"* (my favorite San Francisco restaurant), Mr. Coppola's Zoetrope Cafe, Hilstone (formerly Houston's), and a few "field trips" to Bob's Donuts on Polk Street. In Colorado Springs: Shuga's, Biaggis, Village Inn (Garden of the Gods), Serrano's, Montague's, Poor Richard's, Blue Star (!), and Starbucks No.6392 (Garden of the Gods Road). In Southern Cal, Mí Píacé (Pasadena). I've also doodled on a warehouse-full of butcher paper—thinking out loud at Balthazar (NYC).

Ken Davis pushed me back to my "big desk" to share my work with a broader audience, in print. It's done, Ken (and the next book is well under way)—you can go play with your grandkids.

Danny de Armas, consiglieri and sounding board, has offered outstanding and timely professional advice.

All the corporate and faith-based groups that I have partnered with to HATCH! donuts on *your* moon. A lot of what we learned together is in these pages.

---

1. **Rejection is common in publishing**. The first *rule* of publishing is "Thou shalt be rejected." A lot of famous authors and books were rejected … a lot : *Dr. Seuss* was turned away by 24 publishers; Madeleine L'Engle's *A Wrinkle In Time* by 26; *Harry Potter* by 9; *Gone With the Wind* by 38; *Diary of Anne Frank* by 16; John Grisham's first book, *A Time to Kill,* by 12 publishers (and 16 agents). *Chicken Soup for the Soul,* 140 rejections. Only seven Emily Dickinson poems were published in her lifetime. Then there's this: One editor's rejection letter to Rudyard Kipling said, "Dear Mr. Kipling, I'm sorry, but you just don't know how to use the English language." (No one can recall the name of that editor.)

Herb Hansen & Terry Olson former partners in crime (and comedy) at SAK Theatre. We were a force of nature, creating a lot together with brainstorming as a way of life, and a way of making art.

Marty Sklar, my boss and mentor at Disney Imagineering, who brought me in and booted me out of the "sandbox"—when it was time for me to *grow.* I still have your business card, Marty, on which you scribbled "wish you were here" the night you invited me to be an Imagineer (over dinner at Alfredo's).

A legion of **Imagineering** accomplices who taught me craftsmanship, team work, and the value of saying every idea, *out loud.* I miss *most* of you, but especially: Bob Weis, Joe Rohde, Chris Carradine, Eric Jacobsen, Eric Robison, Andrea Favilli, Dennis Kuba, Eddy Sotto, Tony Baxter, Randy Bright, Alec Scribner, Bill Stout, Jim Steinmeyer, Barry Braverman, Becky Bishop, Tim and Steve Kirk, John Roberdeau Drury, Tom Fitzgerald, Betsy Richman, Bob Gurr, Chick Russell, Christian Hope, Cindy Cote, Dan Nicklason, Dave Fink, Frank and Karen Armitage, Frank Tamura, Hani El-Masri, Jan Sircus, Jeff Kurtti, JoAnn Braheny, Joe Lanzisero, John Hench, Jon Georges, Jon Snoddy, Jim Schull, "K" Rupp, Kathy Kirk, Kathy Mangum, Kathy Rogers, Kevin Rafferty, Larry Gertz, Larry Hitchcock, Larry Nikolai, Lisa Girolami, Maggie Elliot, Matt Priddy, Melody Malmberg, Michael Sprout, Mickey Steinberg, Mike Morris, Mike West, Nancy LaRue, Nina Rae Vaughn, Orlando Ferrante, Peggy Fariss, Peggy Van Pelt, Philip Vaughn, Rich Procter, Randy Printz, Richard Vaughn, Rick Rothschild, Rose Likes, Ryan Harmon, Sandy Vidan (a.k.a. "Miss Preen," my assistant), Steve Miller, Tim Delaney, Tom Morris, Tom Sheroman, Tony Marando, Tori Atencio, Trevor Bryant, Van Romans, Lynn Macer, Barb Dietzel, Zofia Kostryko-Edwards, and the too-soon departed Bruce Gordon and David Mumford. (Thanks to David Fisher for making me Captain of the Mark Twain riverboat for nearly eight years. Love to do it again, David.) And a few Imagineering legends I spent time with and always learned from: Sam McKim, Herb Ryman, Bill Evans, Ward Kimball, Harper Goff, Ken Anderson, Bill Justice, Roy O. Disney (Walt's nephew), Bill Martin, Clem Hall, Collin Campbell, "X" Atencio, Marc Davis, Bill Evans, and Claude Coats.
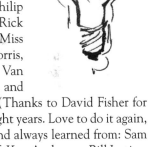

Michael Eisner, Disney CEO, who liked (and paid for) more than a couple of my wacky ideas, even when I wore my Bullwinkle J. Moose lapel pin during a presentation at WDI. (Leading to *Moose & Squirrel* on Disney Video!)

The turn-this-into-an-actual-book part, requires talents and skills I do not practice. Thanks: **Liz Duckworth** who directed me to **Lisa Barnes** (interior design) who pointed me to **Karen Pickering** at Book Villages (publishing and distribution). One of my favorite baristas, **Elizabeth Simpich,** connected me with her brother **Kemper Simpich** (graphic designer) who translated (and improved) my design ideas for front and back covers plus striped spine. My wizard friend **MylesPinkney.com** (you'll see) assisted with preparing my art for print. And **Louis Lemoine** for magical feedback.

"Rabbi Mark" Hurwitz: A long-overdue round of applause to Mark and the other demi-geniuses at Nisus.com for creating the most elegant word processing program on the planet: *Nisus Writer Pro* (Mac only).

Bill Griffis for long, stimulating, creative conversations and providing a home and studio to finish this book and start the next ones.

MaxPaul Franklin for being a professional peer and a sounding board. And for being the first to test *The Fearless Field Guide to Doodling.*

Steve Björkman, a friend since *sixth grade,* for great, encouraging emails and cartoons posted on my Facebook page while I was HATCHing these pages. He also gave me permission to use his sketches (page 165, 192). Steve has inspired me for more than four decades. (www.SteveBjörkman.com)

Jay Ward, Pixar Studios, and **Steve Masseroni,** EA and NVIDIA, who both gave professional council and encouragement for this project.

Gus Dizon, of Industrial Light & Magic and Tippett Studios, for creative conversations in the Bay area and for the likeness of me in action that he dashed off (*below*) during one of my workshops.

Gordon MacKenzie hero to all us "Corporate Conundrums" everywhere.

J. Maxwell Miller with whom I have brainstormed everything from attractions for EPCOT Center to solving the challenge of teaching creativity to Disney executives—a skill we both continue to practice with business leaders everywhere. I am always smarter with Max. His unique balance of playfulness and precision delights me.

Susan Kennedy (a.k.a. SARK), is inside of every page in this book. It could not have happened without her sturdy friendship, professional insight, and buoyant inspiration for the past sixteen years. Whenever I was "stuck" (worried), Susan reminded me to turn to my better instincts and Creator Spirit. Her early enthusiasm for HATCH! sustained me through this project (and many others.) I am blessed to have her in my life.

Donna & **Elwood "Wils" Wilson,** my mom and dad, who were too soon gone from the human neighborhood (1992). They didn't *allow* me to be me, they *encouraged* it. There was never a hint that not getting a straight-A report card was a problem—even when they knew it was within my reach. They taught my brother and me the Truth, early—and set us free. There was always deep, joyous, ferocious Faith in a personal Creator—author of our imaginations. They still inspire me and make me laugh.

My hope is that this book will have the same effect on each reader. **HATCH!** is intended to be the first in a series of three (maybe four) books on creativity and powerful communications in the workplace. The next two books are already in the works—the fourth is an idea that's brewing.

AUTHOR & ILLUSTR◄TOR

C. McNair Wilson :: Is one of the leading voices for creativity in corporate and personal life. His keynote presentations, seminars, and brainstorming coaching have been used by professional groups from Apple, Chick–fil–A, and the Salvation Army, to the Smithsonian Institute. He has worked with associations of attorneys, electricians, doctors, accountants, filmmakers, publishers, pastors, police, bakers, bankers, engineers, and educators.

At Walt Disney Imagineering, McNair was Director of Live Show Design and served on concept & design teams for five new Disney theme parks, resorts, and new attractions for existing parks. Favorite projects include Disney's Hollywood Studios, TOWER of TERROR (for which he lead the original concept team), and PLEASURE ISLAND (especially the Adventurers' Club).

Post–Imagineering McNair developed projects with Universal Studios (Seuss Landing), Warner Bros. (Movie World, Germany), and Sony Entertainment (Metreon, San Francisco).

McNair's "An Imagineer's Behind the Dreams" tours inside Disney theme parks are popular with corporate and non-profit groups—in any Disney theme park.

His previously published books (with his illustrations) include:
- *RAISED IN CAPTIVITY, A Memoir of a Life Long Churchaholic*
- *EVERYONE WANTS TO GO TO HEAVEN, BUT ... Wit, Faith, and a Light Lunch*

His cartoons have marred pages of magazines from *Rolling Stone, Leadership Journal, Decision, Youthworker Journal, Wired, Willow, Wordsmith,* to *The Wittenburg Door.*

McNair's life in the theatre began at age five when he was misbehaving at dinner and his father dismissed him, saying, "Go to your room 'til you learn how to act."

"So, I did."

He has worked with the Children's Theatre Company of Minneapolis, Lamb's Players (San Diego); SAK Theatre Co., Orlando Theatre Project; Theatre Quest (Pasadena, CA, see chapter 12); and the California Shakespeare Theater (Berkeley). He is a member of the Dramatist Guild of playwrights and composers.

McNair by ClarkTate.com

McNair continues to work as a freelance stage director, playwright, actor, artist–in–residence at theatres and colleges. He has performed his original, one–man–plays: *The Fifth Gospel* and *From Up Here* more than 1,500 times.

Follow him on Twitter **@mcnairwilson** or his popular blog **"www.TeaWithMcNair.com"**

His home is wherever he hangs his collection of 230 hats. He actually lives in baggage claim at an international airport (baggage claim carousel No.4).

HATCH! is the first in McNair's three-book series on creativity and communications in professional and personal life.

McNair is available for dinner most nights of the week.

Also by **C. McNair Wilson**, so far
Books
>**YHWH Is Not a Radio Station in Minneapolis** (1983)
>**Everyone Wants To Go To Heaven, But ...** (2001)
>**Raised In Captivity,** *A Memoir of a Life Long Churchaholic* (2003)
>**Straight From the Horses Mouth,** *A-Z Animal Adages* (2008)
>**HATCH!** *Brainstorming Secrets of a Theme Park Designer* (2012)

World Wide Web
> *BLOG on the actively creative life:*
> www.TeaWithMcNair.com
> www.facebook.com/**Hatch-by-McNair-Wilson**
> Facebook: **McNair Wilson International Fan Club** *&* **Dry Cleaning**
> **www.McNairWilson.Com** (Booking Info *&* speaking schedule)
> **Twitter**: @mcnairwilson

Plays & Musicals
> ***I, Witness** - The Story of Jesus from hillside sermon to empty tomb, as told by his friend Levi (2011) Big cast Easter play.
> ***The Good Friday Scenes** (2011) - Three short, two-character, behind-the-story moments designed for Good Friday services. Just add music, lesson/sermon, etc.
> **How the West Was Saved** (1980) Music by Sonny Salisbury
> **Love, You Spoke a Word** (1982) Music by Ken Medema
> ***A Christmas Carol** (adapted from Dickens) (1985)
> *Scripts available from McNair: bigdesk@mcnairwilson.com. Write "Script Request" in subject line.

One-Man Plays
> **The Fifth Gospel** (1972)
> **From Up Here** (1996)
> **Raised In Captivity LIVE!** (2003)

CRE◄TIVI┣Y TO GO
[*other resources*]

 Read Any Good BOOKS Lately?

How To Think Like Leonardo da Vinci by **Michael J. Gelb**. This delight-*full* and engaging look at one of the great genius, artist, scientists—and his seven (7!) principles for success. Great read, fun exercises, with Leonardo as coach.

Making Your Creative Dreams Real by **SARK** (one name like Lassie, Cher, and McNair). Our best creativity coach maps out a fun and practical strategy for making any dream project a reality. (No. 12 of 16 books from SARK.) Find her online at the rich web spot: **www.PlanetSARK.com**.

Walking On Water by **Madeleine L'Engle**. The effulgent author of *A Wrinkle in Time* crafts a rich and compelling case for the nexus of her faith and the art of writing. The only book I have read five times, word-for-word.

Orbiting the Giant Hairball by **Gordon MacKenzie**, Hallmark Card's "creative conundrum" tells tales of freeing your spirit in a corporate environment in this delicious and doodle-full book. *The* best book about expressing creativity in the workplace ... so far. Visually remarkable.

Re-Imagine! by **Tom Peters**. The biggest, most colorful, chock-full-of-goodies book that addresses creativity in our ever-shifting global economy. From the co-author of *In Search of Excellence*.

How You Do Anything Is How You Do Everything by **Cheri Huber & June Shiver**. Cheri's engaging workbook is a self-guided tour through the verdant forest of your life choices. You can open it on any page and GO!

Walt Disney Imagineering: A Behind the Dreams Look At Making the Magic Real Large format and probably the best book on Imagineering—hundreds of illustrations from concept art to never-built ideas.

Rules of the Red Rubber Ball, **Kevin Carroll** reminds us of some of the great playground rules that hold true to this day. Same book designer as *Orbiting the Giant Hairball*, so ... a visual feast with the powerful content.

War of Art by **Stephen Pressfield**. Bite-size chapters on the battle to overcome personal "resistance" in pursuing our personal passions and creative dreams.

Wizard of Ads, **Roy Williams**, top ad-man, author, and seminar leader has an immensely readable and inspiring style to coax us toward mastery in business, PR, and marketing. His Wizard Academy in Austin, Texas, is worth a visit.

ZAG by **Marty Neumeier**. He who has made rule-breaking and WILD Ideas a way of life—and his business—shows us the way to succeed by going against the conventional wisdom. Small book, powerful content, fun read. (Also, **The Brand Gap** and **The Designful Company**)

My favorite biography of **Walt Disney** is the well researched and endlessly readable: **The Animated Man: A Life of Walt Disney** by J. Michael Barrier. It is a balanced, no-hiding-the-warts-or-controversy book with loads of detail of this fascinating life. It is better than Neal Gabler's bio. Barrier has written a shorter, but not short, and fascinating book.

More books for your creative spirit will be recommended as they are released. I post titles on Facebook /Hatch by McNair Wilson and many are already on my blog: **Tea With McNair.**

See also **Further Reading** (page 182) at the end of chapter 14, **The Doodle Factor.**

Right :: My notes (sketch) during a performance
of the play "GALILEO" by Bertolt Brecht
at Belhaven University Theatre, Jackson MS.
Directed by Joseph Frost

NOTES and Doodles

MORE
GREAT
QUESTIONS

THINK
SAY
WRITE
....
NEWSLETTER
OF THE
FUTURE
....
NO
BLOCKING
YES, AND
W!LD
IDEAS
MORE
<><><><><>
DONUTS
ON THE
MOON
<><><><><>
ASSUME
THIS!